For
Susan, Libby, and Henrietta

THE
PENTAGON PAPERS
TRIAL

BY

KENNETH W. SALTER

A JUSTA PUBLICATIONS BOOK

1975

EDITORIAL JUSTA PUBLICATIONS, INC.

P. O. Box 9128
Berkeley, California 94709

First Printing: April 1975

Library of Congress Catalog Card Number: 75-13695

ISBN: 0-915808-00-5

About the Author

Kenneth W. Salter received his J.D. degree from Boalt Hall, the School of Law, University of California at Berkeley in 1967. From 1967–1971 he coordinated pre-law studies and directed the inter-disciplinary freshman composition program in the Department of Speech, University of California, Berkeley. Since 1971 professor Salter has taught pre-law courses and directed field studies in the Department of Speech-Communication, San Jose State University, San Jose, California.

Professor Salter is an Associate Editor of the Barristers *Bailiwick*, a publication of the San Francisco Bar Association. He has written numerous articles on a wide range of subjects related to law and jurisprudence.

Cover Design by Edel A. Villagomez

The Contents

The Sequence of Events

June 17, 1967.   Robert S. McNamara commissions the Pentagon Papers study.

January 21, 1969.   38 volumes of classified Pentagon Papers study deposited with RAND Corporation in Washington, D.C.

February 1969.   Daniel Ellsberg given access to a copy Pentagon Papers study deposited with RAND in Washington, D.C. by Morton Halperin and Leslie Gelb.

March 4, 1969.   Daniel Ellsberg transfers selected volumes of
August 29, 1969.   Pentagon Papers study to RAND in Santa Monica, CA.

October/   Daniel Ellsberg together with Anthony Russo
  November 1969.   and others copy Pentagon Papers study, Wheeler Report and Gertov study in advertising offices of Linda Sinay.

November 1969.   Daniel Ellsberg delivers a copy of Pentagon Papers study to William Fullbright, Chairman of the Foreign Relations Committee of the U.S. Senate.

June 13, 1971.   The New York *Times* obtains most but not all of the narrative history and documents of the Pentagon Papers study and begins publishing them in installments.

The Pentagon Papers Trial

June 16, 1971.   Justice Department obtains a temporary restraining order halting publication, contending that if publication continues "the national defense interests and nation's security will suffer immediate and irreparable harm."

June 30, 1971.   Supreme Court of the U.S. frees newspapers on 6–3 vote to continue publication of the study.

U.S. indites Daniel Ellsberg for theft and espionage in connection with his copying of Pentagon Papers.

August 1971.   Los Angeles grand jury subpoenas Anthony Russo who invokes his Fifth Amendment right to refuse to testify.

August 16, 1971.   Anthony Russo granted immunity from prosecution; must testify or go to jail. Russo cited for contempt of court and goes to jail for six weeks for refusing to testify before the grand jury.

October 1, 1971.   Anthony Russo freed from jail. Government prosecutor, David Nissen, refuses to furnish Russo a copy of the grand jury proceedings.

December 29, 1971.   Grand jury returns second indictment superceding the first and this time charging Anthony Russo as a co-defendant and conspirator with Daniel Ellsberg and others.

July 29, 1972.   Trial proceedings halted after selection of a jury to allow defense appeal to U.S. Supreme Court on Judge Byrne's wiretap ruling.

November 13, 1972.   U.S. Supreme Court by 7–2 vote refuses to hear defendants' case on whether a conversation picked up by the government on a "foreign intelligence" wiretap might impair defendants' right to a fair trial; trial resumes.

December 12, 1972. Judge Byrne officially declares a mistrial in the Pentagon Papers case and orders selection of a new jury to try Ellsberg and Russo.

January 17, 1973. The presentation of opening statements and evidence begins after selection of the second jury.

May 11, 1973. Judge Byrne dismisses the charges against Daniel Ellsberg and Anthony Russo.

Steps in the Federal
Criminal Jury Trial Process

1. The Justice Department Determines To Prosecute.
2. Government Prosecutors Seek An Indictment Before A Federal Grand Jury.
3. The Grand Jury Hears The Government's Witnesses And Votes Whether To Indict.
4. After The Grand Jury Votes To Indict, The Defendant Is Arrested And A Date is Set For Arraignment On The Charges.
5. The Defendant Is Arraigned And Enters His Plea. If He Pleads Guilty, A Date Is Set For Sentencing. If He Pleads Not Guilty And Requests A Jury Trial, A Trial Date Is Set. If The Defendant Prefers To Be Tried Before A Judge, He May Waive Trial By Jury And A Jury And A Trial Before A Judge Is Scheduled.
6. The Defense Attorney(s) File Motions Affecting The Scope of The Trial, eg., To Change The Venue, For Discovery Of Government Witnesses And Documents, For The Suppression of Illegally Obtained Evidence, etc. This Process May Go On For Several Months.
7. A Jury Is Selected.
8. The Government Presents Its Opening Statement.
9. The Defense Presents Its Opening Statement Or Reserves It Until Before The Presentation Of Its Case.
10. The Government Presents Its Case. Government Witnesses Testify And The Defense Cross-Examines. After All Government Witnesses Have Testified, The Prosecution Rests.
11. The Defense Presents Its Case. Defense Witnesses Testify And The Government Cross-Examines.
12. Upon The Conclusion Of The Defense's Case, The Defense

Introduction

BACKGROUND TO THE PENTAGON PAPERS TRIAL

On June 17, 1967 then Secretary of Defense Robert S. Mc-Namara commissioned a top secret study to trace the history of United States involvement in Vietnam from World War II to the present. A team of researchers culled from various sources including universities, the army and other branches of the military, and "think tanks" such as RAND Corporation wrote and compiled the resulting 47-volume study, which was to become known as the "Pentagon Papers". Daniel Ellsberg was one of these researchers. Researchers like Ellsberg who worked only on selected portions of the study, were not permitted to see other parts of the study or to have access to source materials beyond the scope of their assignment. By the end of the Johnson Administration in 1968, only 38 volumes of the Pentagon Papers had actually been typed and of these typed volumes there were only five or six copies in existence. Dr. Morton Halperin, Deputy Assistant Secretary of Defense for Internal Security under Secretary McNamara and the head of the study's task force, retained one set of the study.

Upon leaving government service after the end of the Johnson administration, Halperin arranged to deposit his copy of the Pentagon Papers study, which he shared with two colleagues on the project, in a top secret safe in RAND Corporation's Washington, D.C. office. Daniel Ellsberg, who then worked for RAND at the company's Santa Monica, California offices, learned of the existence of the completed Pentagon Papers study and tried, at first unsuccessfully, to gain access to Halperin's copy. By March 4, 1969, Ellsberg gained access to the 38 typed volumes on deposit with RAND in Washington, D.C. and received permission to transfer the study to his office at RAND in Santa Monica.

Sometime around September 30, 1969, Daniel Ellsberg began secretly to remove volumes of the Pentagon Papers study from his office in Santa Monica and together with Anthony Russo, a former RAND colleague, and Linda Sinay, a friend of Russo's who had access to a Xerox machine in her advertising offices, they copied several volumes of the study along with related documents. Ellsberg returned the copied originals to his office at RAND and redeposited them in his office safe.

Sometime in November 1969 Ellsberg delivered a copy of the Pentagon Papers study to Senator William Fulbright, Chairman of the Foreign Relations Committee of the U.S. Senate, in the hope that Senator Fulbright would schedule committee hearings at which Ellsberg could testify on questions related to this country's involvement in the Vietnam War and related issues. Ellsberg planned to introduce the Pentagon Papers study as exhibits before the committee to support his testimony, hoping, in this way, to make the study available to the press and the public.

But Senator Fulbright's committee did not schedule the hearings, and on June 13, 1971, Ellsberg delivered portions of the study to the New York *Times* for publication. The *Times*, along with other major dailies, began immediately to publish excerpts of the study in daily installments.

The *Times'* publication of excerpts from the classified top secret Pentagon Papers study on June 13, 1971, was the catalyst which set in motion the chain of events that became, in the words of Ellsberg's chief trial counsel, Leonard Boudin, "the political trial of our time" and perhaps more important, it provided the opportunity at last for a historic courtroom encounter on the two great American issues of the last decade: governmental secrecy and the prosecution of the war in Vietnam.

The publication of the Pentagon Papers by the New York *Times* set in motion another set of events that was not to surface publicly until the closing moments of the trial of Ellsberg and Russo itself: the now familiar clandestine activities of the so-called White House "Plumbers." The Plumbers unit headed by White House aides David Young and Egil Krogh and staffed by ex-CIA supersleuth Howard Hunt and ex-FBI undercover operative Gordon Liddy, as well as others, was set-up specifically to stop the "leaks" of top secret and classified documents such as the Pentagon Papers study. Only later, in the closing moments of the trial, was America to learn the full range of the Plumbers' clandestine activities, including the burglary of Daniel Ellsberg's psychiatrist's office in search of privileged, confidential, psychotherapist-patient files for information to undermine and slander Ellsberg's reputation and character. This episode was later to connect the Ellsberg matter directly to Watergate.

Three days after the *Times'* first publication of the still classified, top secret Pentagon Papers, the Justice Department sought and obtained on June 16, 1971, a temporary restraining order which halted for the time being further publication of extracts from the Pentagon Papers. The Justice Department contended that if publication were to continue, "the national defense interests and the nation's security will suffer immediate and irreparable harm."

On June 30, 1971, the United States Supreme Court, by a vote of 6–3, overturned the government's request for a permanent restraining order barring the newspapers from continuing to publish excerpts from the Pentagon Papers. Thus, the Court's vote freed the newspapers to continue publication of the rest of the Pentagon Papers.

On the same day, Daniel Ellsberg was indicted on two counts of theft and espionage in connection with his copying the Pentagon Papers and supplying copies to persons not entitled

3

to receive them. The indictment was careful not to name the
New York *Times* or other newspapers and careful to allege that
the criminal acts specified in the indictment took place in 1969,
when Ellsberg copied the documents, and not to the subsequent
period when he turned the study over to either the Senate committee or the newspapers.

Anthony Russo and Linda Sinay were not indicted along with
Ellsberg. They were instead subpoenaed, in August 1971, by a
federal grand jury in Los Angeles to tell what they knew of the
taking and copying of the documents. Russo refused to testify
before the grand jury and invoked his Fifth Amendment right to
refuse to testify on grounds that he might incriminate himself.
The government countered this tactic by granting him immunity from prosecution in relation to his actions in the copying of
the Pentagon Papers documents, and the court ordered him to
testify or suffer the penalty for contempt of court. Russo perse-
vered in his refusal to testify, was found in contempt of court,
and was sent to jail until such time as he would testify or until
the expiration of the term of the present grand jury whichever
occured first. Russo spent six weeks in jail for his refusal to testify before he was relieved by a federal judge.

Linda Sinay was also called before the grand jury to tell what
she knew of the duplicating of the Pentagon Papers. She, too,
was reluctant to testify and was granted immunity from prosecution. She opted to tell the grand jury about the copying sessions rather than face the possibility of going to jail for contempt
of court. As she later stated to one reporter, "I have two children
and I really didn't want to go to jail. It's that simple. Besides, I
didn't tell them anything they didn't already know."

On December 29, 1971, the federal grand jury returned
a second 15 count indictment, which superseded the earlier 2
count indictment against Ellsberg, and this time the new indictment included Russo as a co-defendant with Daniel Ellsberg.
Ellsberg was charged with five counts of theft, six counts of espionage and both Ellsberg and Russo were charged together

4

with conspiracy to commit theft and espionage. Ellsberg now faced a possible sentence of 105 years in prison if convicted on all counts. Russo was additionally charged with one count of theft and two of espionage. He now faced the prospect of 25 years in prison if convicted on all counts as a reward for his refusal to testify before the grand jury.

By July 29, 1972, a jury was selected to hear the case. But the trial had to be halted to allow for appeal to the United States Supreme Court on the trial judge's ruling that the fact that the government had picked-up a conversation involving defense counsel Boudin on a "foreign intelligence" wiretap did not impair the defendants' right to a fair trial. On November 13, 1972, by a vote of 7–2, the Supreme Court refused to hear the defense's arguments and the trial resumed. Judge Matthew Byrne reluctantly declared a mistrial on December 12, 1972, at the "suggestion" of the 2nd Circuit Court of Appeals that during the five month recess the original jury had had access to too much information affecting the trial and could now be biased by the extensive media coverage of the case. Judge Byrne dismissed the jury and ordered the selection of a new jury to hear the case.

By January 17, 1973, a new jury was empanelled and the presentation of evidence was finally ready to commence. It was now over a year and a half since Ellsberg had first been indicted. When the trial ended abruptly on May 11, 1973, all the evidence had been presented by both sides and the case was ready to go to the jury for their deliberation and determination of the defendants' guilt or innocence. Judge Byrne's dismissal of the charges against Daniel Ellsberg and Anthony Russo, and the circumstances compelling dismissal of the case against the prosecution will be taken up in a companion volume to this book dealing with transcript materials on the question of whether there was an attempt to bribe the trial judge.

The abrupt conclusion to the trial and the judge's dismissal of the charges against the defendants left the question of whether the defendants did in fact "steal" the Pentagon Papers from the government unanswered. The still unresolved issues raised by the theft charges offer a unique opportunity for the student to put himself or herself in the jury box and attempt to resolve and answer the question of guilt or innocence. The charges raise novel issues. Did Daniel Ellsberg and Anthony Russo "steal" the Pentagon Papers? Is it possible to steal information written on a page by copying the document but not by actually keeping the original document? Is it theft to copy documents rightfully in your possession for the purpose of turning them over to elected Senate and Congressional leaders? And is the agreement to copy them conspiracy to commit theft and espionage? Is every government official who "leaks" classified information to the press liable to indictment on the same charges as Ellsberg? And is every newspaperman who receives and prints the classified information liable to the same fate as Russo? These are only some of the important unresolved issues the trial raised that affect our First Amendment freedoms. Because of the abrupt termination of the case they still need resolution. The trial was the first trial to really focus the present dilemma of the right of the press and public to have full access to information and the government's need for secrecy in sensitive foreign policy and national security matters.

The trial also provides a preview and introduction to the Watergate burglary and the resulting political maelstrom which has consumed American political life for the past two years. The still unfolding Watergate saga has given rise to concern over the apparent lack of ethical guidelines and training in American college curricula and in professional graduate schools. The last stages of the trial included the presentation of testimony bearing on the question of whether the offer of the post of Director of the FBI to Judge Byrne by presidential adviser John Ehrlichman while the Pentagon Papers trial was in progress was an attempt to bribe the trial judge and to influence the outcome of the trial. The bribery issue is also one of the charges that the House Judiciary Committee actively investigated in connection with its impeachment inquiry.

THE PARTICIPANTS

The protagonists in the courtroom drama add to the interest the issues in the trial generated. Daniel Ellsberg is still the center of a heated controversy. Was he a patriot who put aside allegiance to his employer, personal ambition, and the cult of secrecy in government to follow the dictates of conscience by releasing the Pentagon Papers as the defense argued, or was he a traitor against whom the government must defend and protect itself? Daniel Ellsberg's real motives for his decision to copy and release the Pentagon Papers have been the source of a continuing controversy in the liberal press. To some of his critics he appears as a forty-year-old neurotic opportunist and hypocrite; to others he is a hero of the anti-war movement. Much of the controversy stems from the fact that Ellsberg's life and work prior to his copying the Pentagon Papers seems inconsistent with the resolve to release the study when he did.

Ellsberg was educated at Harvard University where he received his Ph.D. in economics in 1962. In between his undergraduate and graduate years he served as a rifle company commander in the Marines. From 1959 to 1964, Ellsberg worked as a strategic analyst at RAND Corporation and as a consultant to the Department of Defense. His work during this period was concentrated on problems of strategic nuclear deterrence and Presidential control of nuclear forces. In 1964, he was a researcher on a project sponsored by Walt Rostow, then Chairman of the State Department Policy Planning Council where he was given unprecedented access to highly classified data and studies in order to facilitate his investigation of patterns in high-level

7

decision-making during periods of crisis. Through this work he gained access to studies and data in all government agencies on past crisis decision-making including such episodes as the Cuban missile crisis, Suez invasion, Berlin airlift, and the Gary Powers U-2 incident. Ellsberg's "closed-mouth" stance concerning what he knew as a result of his access to such information was to later cause Russo to remark, after they had fallen-out, "Dan Ellsberg is a cover story. He's so deep into the secrecy system that he can't reveal to himself who he is. It's classified."

In 1965–67, Ellsberg spent two years in Vietnam as a consultant and special assistant to first a general and then to the deputy ambassador. This period of his life is an enigmatic one for his followers and critics alike. Ellsberg then supported the war effort and was actively involved in trying to determine the best way to win the war. Life magazine published a picture of this rising young star of the military-policy complex showing him dressed in battle fatigues, holding a submachine gun poised for military action in Vietnam. What Ellsberg saw as he travelled the backroads of Vietnam was to later effect him greatly.

In the fall of 1967, Ellsberg returned to RAND where he began work on the Pentagon Papers study of U.S. decision-making in Vietnam. In late 1968, in a RAND project for Dr. Henry Kissinger, he co-ordinated a study of a range of policy "options" on Vietnam, and in early 1969 he prepared a study memorandum entitled "National Security Study Memorandum No. 1" which consisted of a set of questions sent to all governmental agencies dealing with Vietnam. He helped summarize the answers to the questions for transmittal to President Nixon who had just assumed office and was re-evaluating the existing Vietnam policy. Shortly after copying the Pentagon Papers, Daniel Ellsberg left RAND Corporation and became a senior research associate at the Center for International Studies at Massachusetts Institute of Technology where he was employed at the time of his indictment.

Anthony Russo worked at the Santa Monica RAND Corporation offices. Russo held a degree in aeronautical engineering from Virginia Polytechnic Institute and had worked for NASA before coming to RAND. Russo also had a degree in international affairs from Princeton. He spent 24 months in Vietnam on various RAND Corporation projects and had the opportunity to interview captured Vietcong and North Vietnamese prisoners for a classified study called the "Vietcong Motivation and Morale Project." It was upon his return from Vietnam that Russo got to know Ellsberg at RAND and they became good friends. Both Russo and Ellsberg were drawn together by the fact that they were among only a handful of RAND policy analysts who had actually spent considerable time inside Vietnam. It was this coincidence that was to lead them both to the gradual discovery that the war in Vietnam was based on "lies, deception, and secrecy" and to convince Ellsberg, who was one of only a few persons to have read the Pentagon Papers in their entirety, that if the Pentagon Papers study was not made public, the Nixon administration might find another pretext for again escalating the war.

The defense attorneys were notable for their experience in utilizing the jury trial as a forum to educate both the jury and the American public to the political and moral issues that underlay the alleged criminal conduct of their clients. Daniel Ellsberg's chief defense attorney, Leonard Boudin, had served as Dr. Spock's attorney and had also served as attorney for Eqbal Ahmad at the Harrisburg conspiracy trial. Charles Nesson, who was a young Harvard Law School professor, and Dolores Donovan, an ACLU lawyer from San Francisco who specialized in defending GI's in military trials in Vietnam, also represented Ellsberg. Russo's principal attorney, Leonard Weinglass, had been co-counsel with William Kunstler for the defendants in the Chicago Eight trial and Judge Hoffman had made him the butt of much derision during the course of the trial. Russo's junior defense counsel was Peter Young.

Judge Matthew Byrne, Jr., was the same age as Ellsberg and

was the son of a federal judge who still presided over a court-room just down the hall. The younger Judge Byrne had been a former prosecuting attorney and had all the credentials to advance further in the judiciary or, if fate had decreed otherwise, to a post in the Justice Department. The FBI is part of the Justice Department.

The prosecution was headed by David Nissen (not to be confused with defense attorney Charles Nesson), a controversial government prosecutor whose refusal to divulge government information relevant to the trial was to be the source of repeated defense allegations of governmental and prosecutorial misconduct..

THE TEXT

While the book was designed primarily as a textbook to facilitate the study of the jury trial system in college classrooms, it was also intended to be a book that would be of interest to the general reader concerned with the resolution of the controversial problems and issues posed by the trial. The text combines the salient portions of the trial transcript on the issue of whether Daniel Ellsberg and Anthony Russo "stole" the Pentagon Papers from the government. The charges in the indictment, the prosecution and defense opening statements, and the evidence presented by both sides that bear on the charges of theft are included in this section. At the end of each section there are a series of questions for classroom discussion and suggested assignments. The questions are also designed for use as guides for jury simulation. The class can be divided into groups of 6, 8, or 12 student-jurors whose function is to determine the guilt or innocence of the defendants solely on the charges of theft that are enumerated in the indictment. Since the case was dismissed by the judge before it could go to the jury for deliberation, the thorny issue of whether the defendants committed theft by removing and copying the documents has not been answered.

Due to space limitations, the evidence presented on the charges of conspiracy and espionage have been omitted. These charges were the most difficult for the prosecution to substantiate on the evidence available. The espionage charges also involved hundreds of pages of testimony of witnesses on both sides as to whether the Pentagon Papers would have been either useful or to the advantage of a hypothetical foreign intelligence analyst.

The author has attempted to present in this volume the theft in the actual context of the trial process itself. The student-juror and general reader is given the requisite framework and evidence from which to make his or her own judgment on the guilt or innocence of the two defendants on the charges of theft, and to assess Ellsberg's and Russo's criminal and moral responsibility, as well as the underlying issues raised by the trial, the trial process, and ultimately the law of theft itself.

The portions of the transcript used in the text are selected and edited from the 130 volumes of actual trial transcript and the over forty volumes of supporting briefs, documents, and other trial related materials. The author wishes to express his appreciation to the Meiklejohn Civil Liberties Institute in Berkeley, California for making available to him its copy of the trial transcript and supporting materials.

JURY DELIBERATION

The questions for discussion and analysis throughout the text are designed to provide a framework for class discussion of the case as well as the framework for mock jury deliberations and/or a mock trial of the case by the class. The learning unit is constructed to cover three to four weeks of class time. The format for mock jury deliberations is to discuss the text for the first 4 to 6 class meetings to identify the issues and familiarize the class with the charges in the indictment and the testimony by the opposing sides.

Upon completion of class discussion, the class is randomly divided into groups of six, eight or twelve jurors. Each student jury is instructed to elect a foreman or forewoman and to review the charges in the indictment. The juries then deliberate their verdict using the questions for discussion and analysis as their guideline. Each jury is instructed to apply the definitions of theft, conversion and embezzlement to the charges in the indictment and to assess the evidence pro and con. The foreperson should attempt to identify the issues of fact that the jury must decide in order to arrive at a verdict on each count in the indictment, e.g. whether Halperin or the government "owned" the Pentagon Papers documents at the time Ellsberg copied them.

When each jury has arrived at a unanimous verdict of guilty or not guilty, a written vote on each count in the indictment is delivered to the instructor who serves as the judge. If the jury is deadlocked on any of the counts in the indictment at the end of the period assigned for jury deliberations, a mistrial is declared by the instructor as to that count. After all juries have reported their verdicts, the results are posted on the blackboard and the class is invited to assess its jury deliberation experience.

MOCK JURY TRIAL

Another approach would be to divide the class into teams of prosecutors, defense attorneys, witnesses and a jury with the instructor to serve as judge. The prosecution and defense teams would conduct the trial based on the information and the format in the text. Each team would add a closing statement to the textual material before giving the case to the jury.

JURY INSTRUCTIONS

Each jury should be charged that the burden of proof is on the government to prove *beyond a reasonable doubt* that the defendants committed the crimes charged in the Indictment. If a juror has a reasonable doubt whether the defendants are guilty as charged, they must be acquitted on that charge.

The Indictment

Daniel Ellsberg and Anthony Russo, Jr., were charged in a 15 count indictment filed on December 30, 1971. The first count, conspiracy, included both defendants. Daniel Ellsberg was charged separately with five counts of theft and six counts of espionage. Anthony Russo was charged with one count of theft and two counts of espionage. Ellsberg faced at the end of the prosecution's case a possible sentence of 105 years in prison and $110,000 in fines if convicted; Russo faced the possibility of 25 years in prison and $30,000 in fines.

Only Counts Two, Three, Four, Five and Six which charge Ellsberg with theft and conversion and Count Seven which charges Russo with receiving stolen goods are reproduced here. The Counts charging joint conspiracy and individual acts of espionage have been omitted.

COUNT TWO

[18 U.S.C. Section 641]

During the period from about March 4, 1969, to about May 20, 1970, in Los Angeles County, within the Central District of California, defendant DANIEL ELLSBERG did embezzle, steal and knowingly convert to his use and the use of another the following things of value of the United States and a department and agency thereof:

14

(1) Nine volumes of a 38-volume Department of Defense study entitled "UNITED STATES-VIETNAM RELATIONS 1945–1967":

Volume	Title
I	VIETNAM AND THE UNITED STATES–1940–1950.
IV.A.2	AID FOR FRANCE IN INDOCHINA–1950–1954.
IV.B.5	EVOLUTION OF THE WAR–The Overthrow of Ngo Dinh Diem–May–November, 1963.
IV.C.4	EVOLUTION OF THE WAR–MARINE COMBAT UNITS GO TO DA NANG–MARCH 1965.
IV.C.5	PHASE I IN THE BUILD-UP OF U.S. FORCES– THE DEBATE MARCH–JULY 1965.
IV.C.8	RE-EMPHASIS ON PACIFICATION: 1965–1967.
IV.C.9(A)	EVOLUTION OF THE WAR–U.S./GVN Relations: 1963–1967–PART II.
VI.C.6	SETTLEMENT OF THE CONFLICT–Negotiations, 1967–1968–HISTORY OF CONTACTS.

(2) Pages 1, 2, 3, 4, 9, 12, 13, and 14 of a memorandum dated 27 February, 1968 entitled "REPORT OF CHAIRMAN, JCS ON SITUATION IN VIETNAM AND MACV FORCE REQUIRE-MENTS;"

(3) Part II of a memorandum entitled "NEGOTIATIONS AND VIETNAM: A CASE STUDY OF THE 1954 GENEVA CON-FERENCE,";

which things had a value in excess of $100;

In violation of Title 18, United States Code, Section 641.

COUNT THREE

[18 U.S.C. Section 641]

During the period from about March 4, 1969, to about May 20, 1970, in Los Angeles County, within the Central District of California, defendant DANIEL ELLSBERG did conceal and retain the following things of value of the United States and a department and agency thereof, with intent to convert them to his own use and gain, knowing them to have been embezzled, stolen, and converted:

Itemization of documents same as in Count Two omitted.

COUNT FOUR

[18 U.S.C. Section 641]

During the period from about March 4, 1969, to about May 20, 1970, in Los Angeles County, within the Central District of California, defendant DANIEL ELLSBERG, without authority, did knowingly convey to Anthony Joseph Russo, the following things of value of the United States and a department and agency thereof:
Itemization of documents same as in Count Two omitted.
In violation of Title 18, United States Code, Section 641.

COUNT FIVE

[18 U.S.C. Section 641]

During the period from about March 4, 1969, to about December 31, 1969, in Los Angeles County, within the Central District of California, defendant DANIEL ELLSBERG, without authority, did knowingly convey to Linda Sinay the following thing of value of the United States and a department and agency thereof: one volume of a 38-volume Department Defense study

16

entitled "UNITED STATES-VIETNAM RELATIONS 1945–1967"; namely, Volume IV.C. 9(b), *"EVOLUTION OF THE WAR-US/GVN Relations: 1963–1967* - PART II," which thing had a value in excess of $100;

In violation of Title 18, United States Code, Section 641.

Itemization of documents same as in Count Two omitted.

COUNT SEVEN

[18 U.S.C. Section 641]

During the period from about March 4, 1969, to about May 20, 1970, in Los Angeles County, within the Central District of California, defendant ANTHONY JOSEPH RUSSO did receive the following things of value of the United States and a department and agency thereof, with intent to convert them to his own use and gain, knowing them to have been embezzled, stolen and converted:

Itemization of documents listed in (1) and (2) of Count Two omitted.

In violation of Title 18, United States Code, Section 641.

Questions for Analysis

The Indictment

Definition of To Steal (Black's Law Dictionary) :

a) the wilful and intentional taking and carrying away of the property of another, and without right and without leave or consent of the owner.

b) the wrongful taking of the property of another without his consent and against his will, with the intent to convert it to the use of the taker.

Definition of Embezzlement (Black's Law Dictionary) :

The fraudulent appropriation of property by a person to whom it has been entrusted, or to whose hands it has lawfully come.

1. Why does the government allege in Count Two that Ellsberg did "embezzle, steal and knowingly convert to his use"? By applying the above definitions of "to embezzle", "to steal", and "to convert", what are the essential differences in the form of action encompassed in each term?

2. Does the government allege in Count Two that Ellsberg stole government property? What is the significance of the allegation that the Pentagon Papers' study has a value in excess of $100.00?

3. How does the criminal act charged in Count Three differ from the criminal acts charged in Count Two? If Ellsberg were to be acquitted of the charges in Count Two, could he still be found guilty of the charge in Count Three?

18

4. How do the criminal acts charged in Counts Four and Five differ from the acts charged in Counts Two and Three? Can Ellsberg be guilty of Count Four or Five and not guilty of Count Two or Three?

5. What criminal act (s) has Russo committed according to the charge in Count Seven? How does the charge against Russo differ from the charges against Ellsberg?

IN THE UNITED STATES DISTRICT COURT
CENTRAL DISTRICT OF CALIFORNIA

———

HONORABLE WM. MATTHEW BYRNE, JR.,
JUDGE PRESIDING

———

UNITED STATES OF AMERICA,)
)
                    Plaintiff,)
)
       vs.   )
)
ANTHONY JOSEPH RUSSO, JR.,)
DANIEL ELLSBERG,   )
)
                 Defendants)

APPEARANCES:

For the Plaintiff:

                              WILLIAM D. KELLER
                              United States Attorney

                              DAVID NISSEN
                              Assistant United States Attorney

                              WARREN REESE
                              Assistant United States Attorney

                              RICHARD BARRY
                              Assistant United States Attorney

For Defendant Russo: LEONARD I. WEINGLASS
                              H. PETER YOUNG

For Defendant Ellsberg: LEONARD B. BOUDIN
                              CHARLES NESSON
                              CHARLES E. GOODELL
                              DOLORES A. DONOVAN

The Government's Opening Statement

BY MR. NISSEN:

That brings me to the subject of the defendants' conduct.

Defendant Ellsberg obtained possession of each of these three items*, ostensibly in connection with his work.

Mr. Russo, the other defendant, was not authorized to have access to them, even when he had been working at Rand earlier, because he had no duties at all which required his access to them.

And, as I say, by the time the documents were taken and the offences committed, he was not working at Rand.

On March 3, 1969, under a Rand letter which appointed him as a courier, between its Washington, D.C. sub-office and its home office in Santa Monica, Mr. Ellsberg appeared at the Washington office of Rand and obtained ten volumes of the eighteen volumes that we are discussing. That's March 3, '69.

At that time, and before he was allowed to take them, he was required to sign a receipt which stated, in sub-

---

* The 3 items referred to and listed in the indictment were the Pentagon Papers, the Gurtov memorandum and Wheeler report.

21

stance, "I certify that I will not copy, reproduce these records," et cetera.

Thereafter on August 28, 1969, again in the Washington suboffice, again with a similar letter, defendant Ellsberg obtained eight other study volumes, the total by that time being eighteen. Again he promised not to copy them, in writing in a certificate.

Now in direct violation of the Industrial Security Manual and the Rand Security Manual and contrary to what he had promised in his memos to the security officer, Mr. Ellsberg failed to deliver those eighteen volumes to the Rand Santa Monica Top Secret Control Officer so that they could be entered into the Rand records of control. Instead he kept them outside someplace for himself.

He retained them until May 20, 1970, a little over a year later. And you will hear how they were ultimately regathered by Rand, through another Rand employee.

The Gurtov document was checked out on April 7, 1969, by defendant Ellsberg from the Top Secret Control Officer at Rand Santa Monica. And that document, likewise, was not returned to Rand until May 20, 1970, a little over a year.

The Wheeler report was checked out from the Top Secret Control Officer at Rand Santa Monica on October 3, 1969, by defendant Ellsberg, and it was returned two weeks later on October 17, 1969.

Now the two defendants, Russo and Ellsberg, decided to copy these and other classified documents. They asked a person named Lynda Sinay for the use of the Xerox machine in her office, and she agreed.

She at that time was the girlfriend of defendant Russo. She is still a close friend of both defendants and is named in the indictment as an unindicted, uncharged, co-conspirator.

Mr. Ellsberg said that he had material from his vault at Rand that he wanted to copy relating to the Vietnam war, he was going to leave Rand or was thinking of leaving, and he wanted to take it with him. He also mentioned that Senator Fulbright might like to see them.

On several occasions over a period of time Miss Sinay's office was used for this copying. Typically defendant Ellsberg would bring the documents to be copied into the office, and would take them and the copies out, but on some occasions the copies may have gone with Mr. Russo.

Defendant Russo, Miss Sinay, defendant Ellsberg, and Mr. Ellsberg's thirteen-year-old son, all participated in copying the top secret documents.

At that time Mr. Ellsberg's girlfriend, Kimberly Rosenberg, was present in the offices, his friend Vu Van Thai, also an unindicted co-conspirator, was present on occasion.

In the offices of Miss Sinay defendant Ellsberg's children were used to cut the top secret markings from the top and bottom of the documents.

Also participating in the project was Miss Sinay herself and the two defendants. And it was obviously done so that it would hide from someone who should look at them or casually look at them the true nature of the documents.

Mr. Ellsberg paid Miss Sinay for the use of her copying machine, by the way. . . .

Now the defendant Ellsberg's copying and furnishing of these top secret documents to defendant Russo, co-conspirator Sinay and Thai, to his son and to other people, was in direct violation of a long list of rules and requirements that he had promised to obey.

One was the Industrial Security Manual; one was the Rand Security Manual; one was the security acknowledgment which was a condition of his employment; one was his certificate on the receipt for the documents when he obtained them that he would not copy them and so forth; the Presidential Executive Order 10501; as well as the federal criminal laws involved.

Both defendants, Russo and Ellsberg, knew of all

these regulations and of the provisions of federal criminal law that dealt with these documents at the time they committed their unlawful acts.

Each volume was stamped prominently in the front with a warning, and I can't quote it exactly, because I don't have it in front of me, but it warned anyone that transmission of the document to an unauthorized person would be a violation of law, because it was a document relating to the national defense.

Secondly, the materials that they received at Rand, including the security acknowledgment that they signed, carried prominently displayed the full text of all the applicable law which they were under and which they signed that they would obey.

It is also obvious from the evidence that they were fully aware that they were violating the law, from merely the way they acted, cutting off the classifications, and, inadvertently while at work in the office, the silent burglar alarm was triggered on a couple of occasions, at least, and the police came to the door, and the defendants were in panic, because they knew that they were doing something that the law forbade. . . .

Now, evidence from the FBI laboratory will reveal that examination of these documents shows latent fingerprints of the people who I have been naming to you, along with the prints of defendant Ellsberg. Only defendant Ellsberg was authorized to possess the documents, and he only in connection with his official duties, which required his access. He had no authority to possess them for the purpose of copying them, which was strictly forbidden, or for the purpose of passing them to Sinay, Thai, his son, Russo, or anybody else.

That is basically the broad picture of the case as you will hear it. . . .

(8268–8339)

Defendant Ellsberg's Opening Statement

THE DEFENSE'S VIEW OF THE
THEFT CHARGE FROM THE OPENING STATEMENT
FOR DEFENDANT ELLSBERG*

BY MR. BOUDIN:

Now let's take these charges, but let's take them in the wrong order, because it is a little easier to do logically.

The charge of theft: This is a charge of theft, as we will show, for giving information or documents to the Congress of the United States.

It is not a charge of theft for personal advantage, for the advantage of a foreign country, for the advantage of a third party.

This is a charge based on the theory that somehow or other, if you take information, let's assume relating—that it is government property for the moment, and you give it to the Congress of the United States, you are taking it away from the government, the theory apparently being that the President is the government and Congress is not.

This is the real basis of the theft charge, the theft of giving information and documents to the Congress of the United States, as the defendant will testify, at least as one of

---

* Upon the conclusion of Mr. Nissen's opening statement for the government, the defense has the opportunity to present its opening statement(s) to the jury with the overview of the case. Mr. Weinglass, Mr. Russo's attorney, chose to reserve his opening statement for the start of the defense's case and presentation of defense witnesses. See infra on page 62.

them will testify, I assume. I can only speak for my client at the moment.

Now it isn't clear, on looking at the indictment, whether the Government is charging the defendants with the theft of information or documents. . . .

Now the Government has talked about documents throughout this as if the documents were owned by the Government. . .that there is considerable doubt whether any of these papers, treating them now as documents, belong to the Government of the United States, their property.

I know the cost that was discussed and how many people worked on it. The question is not how much it costs. The question is to whom did these papers belong. . . .

To whom did the information in the Pentagon Papers belong? To the government of the United States? Or didn't it belong to the people of the United States and the Senate Committee on Foreign Relations representing the Congress and dealing with our foreign policy?

And we will attempt to show you that this information, because of its character, because it didn't deal with military operations, but dealt with how we got into a war, and possibly how we could get out of it, that this information was the property of the government, and the government wasn't the one the gentlemen are referring to.

The goverment was the Congress of the United States to whom it went, shortly after it was copied, a fact we are going to admit in a few minutes.

We will also show that it couldn't have been government property for a completely different reason: It was improperly classified.

Now you heard the Government say in the opening that when a document is classified that proves it belongs to the Government, but it is not going to prove by witnesses that it is properly classified.

We dispute that. We think the Government has to

prove that it is properly classified.

But we are not going to wait for somebody to decide this. We are going to put on witnesses who will testify that these particular Pentagon Papers should never have been classified because they don't meet the standards of Executive Order 10501, the Executive Order referred to by Mr. Nissen. . . .

We will also show that much—I don't say all, it will depend on what the Government wants to put in and how it expects to prove it—that much of the material which is in the indictment from the Pentagon Papers appears in contemporaneous newspaper reports.

You might have to go to Canada to read them, or subscribe to a Canadian newspaper, or to a French newspaper like Le Monde, or an English newspaper.

But it was there, and it was there before the acts of copying which are the bases of the charges here.

In other words, we are going to argue and prove to you that these things were in what we call the public domain, and that when the Government prosecutes here it is prosecuting for exactly the kind of thing that it itself gives to the press.

Surprising, but we will prove it. . . .

Dr. Ellsberg's possession of the Pentagon Papers was lawful, and we will show, from official records of the Rand Corporation that, as a matter of fact, from the time he received the papers in Washington, D.C., these Pentagon Papers, which he got in the spring and fall of 1969, according to the government's—according to the Rand's own top secret control office's affidavit, that he was the only person—only person authorized to have possession of and access to these documents, talking now about the Pentagon Papers.

Now, I am not suggesting, if I suggested it earlier —one of my colleagues thought I did—that Dr. Ellsberg complied with all the rules and regulations of the Rand Corporation. I didn't mean to say that. Rand didn't tell him to go out and copy the documents.

What I am saying is that that didn't stop his possession from being lawful. He was still the only one who had lawful possession. If he violated the rules, then there are ways under the Rand contract, and under the Rand Manual, assuming it is relevant here at all in a criminal case—there are ways of taking care of employees who violate rules.

The argument of the government that he should have brought them immediately from Washington and put them into the Rand security contract machinery, we will show you, was all wrong, a misconception, but it is the basis of their case . . . .

Now let's come to the Pentagon Papers. The Pentagon Papers has origin in a decision by . . . . Secretary of Defense Robert McNamara, who was one of the leaders in this war. . . .

And in 1967, a year that all of us will remember as a year of turmoil in this country and division, Mr. McNamara decided that a study ought to be made of the history of the United States involvement in Vietnam, from World War II to the present, a study of the history.

Now the reasons for the study, as I say, were inherent in the political situation in 1967, involved questions of why did we get into the war, why are we still there, what mistakes were made—questions that many of you on voir dire I think were asking, and that we are asking. . . .

A team was assembled.* A word has been said about this team, but it was not a team of particularly military men, although there were men from the army, some military men in it.

They were researchers. And the research group was described by Gelb as coming from various categories,

---

* Dr. Morton Halperin who was Deputy Assistant Secretary of Defense, was chosen by McNamara to head the study and Dr. Leslie Gelb was appointed director of the study task force.

universities, think tanks like Rand.

And they came and were given assignments to do work, very often duplicating the work. They were dealing with the same historical periods, overlapping to some extent.

And they did, although they were scholars of different political points of view, they did this quite extraordinary, this unique study, of the United States' involvment in Vietnam.

One of the people, incidentally, who worked on the study, was Dr. Ellsberg. He didn't work on the whole study. He worked on maybe one or more of the volumes.

Now this study was authorized in 1967.

And at the end of the Johnson Administration, in 1968, while forty-seven—sometimes we say forty-eight volumes had been completed, only thirty-seven or thirty-eight had been typed. And there were five or six copies of this Pentagon Papers study, as the core of this case.

Now we will establish by evidence, documentary, witnesses, and so forth, that it is the practice of retiring government officials, from presidents down, whether their names are Truman or Eisenhower or Johnson, and those who eventually leave, the practice of presidents down, and assistant secretaries of state and deputy assistant secretaries and people who held other positions, even lower, it is the practice to take with them when they leave the government their private papers.

And private papers has a very large definition, very large when you are president, and large no matter who you are if you are in the government. You take with you government papers on which you have worked. This is routine.

And large presidential libraries, like the Truman library and the Johnson library, are built upon these thousands and thousands of government files by retiring officials. Nothing wrong with it. It's fine. It is the practice.

Nobody says anybody is stealing anything. Nobody says you are violating the espionage laws. Nobody says you are violating the conspiracy laws. You do it.

And so when these volumes were—when this Johnson Administration was coming to an end, the people who were in the Department of Defense, responsible for this study, decided that they would take their private papers, including at least one copy of this study, with them when they left, because the Nixon Administration was coming in. . . .

And so on December 18, 1968, Mr. Warnke—this is on the stationery of Assistant Secretary of Defense—Mr. Halperin and Mr. Gelb, sent their memorandum to Mr. Harry Rowen, formerly also an official of the Department of Defense, with respect to the distribution of their papers, including what they call the OSD Task Force and related matters.

And what they said was, essentially, and what they did, was that these papers, this Pentagon government study, was going to be deposited in the Rand Washington,D.C., office; and that Paul Warnke, Morton Halperin, Leslie Gelb, are to be the ones who are going to decide who will have access to them.

And so these papers were then, together with all the papers of Mr. McNaughton, who, unfortunately, had died with family in an air crash sometime before, their private papers, the Halperin private papers, some Gelb's possibly—I am not sure now—and the Pentagon Papers were stored in Rand, Washington, D.C. There was a receipt given, and there they were.

They were not given to Rand, remember, for Rand to work on a contract basis; they were left at Rand for the convenience of these government officials who were shortly going to retire.

Now, then came Dr. Ellsberg on the scene, allegedly, according to the government's indictment, pursuant to a conspiracy, that Dr. Ellsberg was going to work at Rand, with which he was still connected, on a study of the lessons to be learned from the Vietnam war, from this particular study. . . .

He was interested in the lessons to be learned,

and he was going to do a monograph or study at Rand on this, so his purpose, notwithstanding the implications of this indictment, was perfectly legitimate and was not secret.

As a result, I believe Mr. Rowen's—Mr. Rowen is the president of Rand in Santa Monica—request to two of the three people, Gelb, Warnke and Halperin—consent was given by those people to have the papers, over which they had control; they had authority; they had taken them out of the government —to have those papers delivered to Dr. Ellsberg so that he could take them to Santa Monica, where he could work on them at the Rand office.

So the people who had the power to authorize delivery and possession, authorized delivery and possession to Dr. Ellsberg.

Dr. Ellsberg took those papers and took them to Santa Monica, both in the spring of 1969 and in the fall, and, as I have told you before, although his purpose was perfectly legitimate, it happens that Mr. Russo was not around and didn't know anything about it, and that Miss Sinay didn't know anything about it; Mr. Vu Van Thai didn't know about it.

Mr. Ellsberg then sat down in Santa Monica and began to read these papers. You know something of his background—perhaps I shouldn't add this, and we should simply offer evidence as to his further experiences, and that is, his actual experiences as a participant in combat operations and his experiences in traveling through thirty-eight of the forty-three provinces in Vietnam—but, at any rate, he read all of these volumes, or many of them, and the volumes told him a great deal.

Now, remember; he had been a participant in the early days, assisting the White House and the National Security Council in policy making; he knew a great many of these things, but he didn't know all of them. He didn't realize the origins of the war, the early history of this war, and there were many lessons which he learned from the Pentagon Papers. . . .

As I say, Dr. Ellsberg felt a special responsibility

31

when he was reading these things, because he has been in the government; he had been doing these things in Vietnam, in the Defense Department, and he was not then a government employee, strictly speaking, but he was bound by the code of ethics, which the Congress of the United States had passed in 1958, which put loyalty to the highest moral principles into country above loyalty to persons, party or government department. He was bound by that, a resolution of Congress.

Dr. Ellsberg also knew, as we will establish here, quite aside from the Pentagon Papers, the Senate Foreign Relations Committee had been battling with the executive, one adminisration after another, to try to get facts about the war. This was long before it knew about these papers, and the Executive Branch, the Department of Defense, said, "No. No. No. Secret, executive privilege, classified; secret, executive privilege, classified" to the Congress of the United States.

Dr. Ellsberg at this time, at this very time, and, indeed, for a—some year or two before that, had become concerned, together with other employees at Rand, who were experts in the war, about the progress of the war, and we will show you that he was in communication with the Carnegie Endowment for International Peace, and its leading official, Charles Bolte, urging a conference of citizens to speak and act in support of the President's proposition "The time has come to end this war." This was on September 23, 1969.

Remember the period of conspiracy alleged in the indictment, from March 1, 1969, to September 30, 1970.

Mr. Bolte sent, showing you the linkage here, Dr. Ellsberg's letter to Senator Fulbright; the Foreign Relations Committee invited Dr. Ellsberg to appear before the committee; the appearance was postponed; Dr. Ellsberg had planned to deliver physically, as you will see, these Pentagon Papers to the committee, and it was the plan—and we believe of some of the committee staff—ultimately to hold hearings on the Pentagon Papers and on the decision-making process of the Executive Branch.

. . . Now, Dr. Ellsberg discussed this matter with Mr. Russo. Mr. Russo's background, I have given you. He was a trusted friend by that time of Dr. Ellsberg, and Mr. Russo agreed to help Dr. Ellsberg find a place where these papers could be Xeroxed, because how could they be gotten to the Senate Foreign Relations Committee, unless you were to steal the copies from Rand, where they were, and so Miss Sinay's place was found, and the papers were taken there overnight and were Xeroxed, and the Pentagon Papers were then returned the next morning to Rand.

Rand still has—except, as I say, they may have been given to the Department of Defense—the original papers that were Xeroxed.

Counsel for the government has made reference to the fact that some of—one or more of Dr. Ellsberg's children was at the Xeroxing process and may have participated in it.

Dr. Ellsberg will explain to you, if he takes the stand—and I assume he will—that he felt he was doing an important thing for his country, and that he wanted his children to know exactly what he was doing, why he was doing it.

Reference has been made by the government to the fact that the words "Top Secret" were cut off some of these papers. An explanation will be given that the fact was that it was envisaged that this was an emergency thing to get these things Xeroxed at once, and if it were going to be given to the Senate Foreign Relations Committee, multiple copies would have to be made in commercial places, which might well be reluctant to Xerox things that are marked "Top Secret."

And so this process occurred; the papers were taken out of Rand—Remember; they were in Dr. Ellsberg's authorized possession; they were Xeroxed; they were returned to Rand, and the Xerox copies were given to Senator Fulbright. That was the plan. That was the intent. That was the reason.

And on November 3, a substantial portion of those papers was given to Senator Fulbright.

On receipt of those papers, Senator Fulbright,

within a few days, immediately wrote the Secretary of Defense Laird, from whom he had been trying to get many, many other papers, and asked Secretary of Defense Laird for the entire set of Pentagon Papers.

We will introduce the letter into evidence at the proper time.

In the letter to Secretary Laird on November 9, 1969, Senator Fulbright said, essentially what we are saying in this case, that the study could be of significant value to the Committee in its review of the Vietnam policy issues, and he appreciated making it available.

Then came months after months of correspondence between Secretary Laird and Senator Fulbright. Secretary Laird refused to give it to the Senate Foreign Relations Committee.

Now, the Foreign Relations Committee eventually got the whole set, but, as you know, it got it only after the publication in the New York Times,* of the Papers, and after repeated demands being—

THE COURT: Stay within the time periods involved in the indictment.

MR. BOUDIN: Yes, your Honor.

Now, you will be reading these papers, and you will probably agree with the government that they are a source of political embarrassment to the government, but you will not come to the conclusion that they have embarrassed the United States militarily; they embarrassed any executive that is seeking to get money and to send soldiers abroad, and who doesn't want to state the true reasons for the continuation of a war.

They will embarrass a government, because the Papers will reveal, not only the political facts that I have described—but the Papers will reveal that the Congress of the

---

* Excerpts of the Pentagon Papers study were published by the New York Times beginning June 13, 1971.

United States and you were deceived by public statements made by executive officials repeatedly. . . .

Now, we don't have to speculate as to whether the National defense was damaged in the slightest, even if Anthony Russo helped Dr. Ellsberg, through Miss Sinay, Xerox some of those documents. We don't have to speculate on whether the United States was endangered at all, even if Mr. Vu Van Thai had a chance to read a few of these pages. We don't have to speculate on whether national defense was injured by giving the papers to Senator Fulbright.*

The fact is that you will come to the conclusion, with or without the experts, that the revelation of this information to your senators and your congressmen was helpful to the interests of the United States and was important that they should have it as your elected representatives.

You will see that it gave Congress, for the first time—maybe there have been fifty years ago; I don't know—an inside look into how presidents and secretaries of state and secretaries of defense really operate, and how they try to manipulate public opinion, and how they actually say to one another, "Let's do this, because this is the right time to affect Congress; let's present it this way, so the public won't realize that we are really accelerating the war; we will say we are following the same old policy with slight modifications."

These Papers explain to Congress what it had long suspected, namely, that it had been deceived, and that you had been deceived, and as a matter of fact, after the Papers reached Senator Fulbright, he moved successfully to repeal the Tonkin Bay Resolution, as you may remember that Senators Gruening and Morris claimed the Congress had been deceived into passing, a step which escalated the war.

. . . All I can say then is that the defendants

----

* The issue whether release of the Pentagon Papers injured the national defense relates only to the conspiracy and espionage charges.

wanted to accomplish the result, not only of telling the public about the war, but fighting the principle of secrecy in the Government, and of showing the absurdity of a classification program that makes absolutely no sense except that it gave a hundred thousand people the right to stamp top secret or secret or otherwise.

The Government, as the court will tell you, has the burden of proving the defendants' guilt beyond a reasonable doubt. The Government has to prove the conspiracy.

It has to prove the theft. It has to prove the violation of the espionage laws.

It has to prove that the acts were willfully done.

The Government has charged unauthorized possession. It has got to prove unauthorized possession.

Thank you.

THE COURT: Thank you, Mr. Boudin.

(8340–8400)

Questions for Study and Analysis

OPENING STATEMENTS

The function of the opening statement in criminal cases is to give the prosecution and defense lawyers an opportunity to present their overview of the case to the jury so that the jury understands how the testimony of each witness relates to the charges in the indictment and what each side must prove as a part of their case. The opening statement is also used to familiarize the jury with the evidence and testimony it will see and hear. The burden of proof is on the prosecution to prove beyond a reasonable doubt that the defendants committed the crime as charged in the indictment.

1. What are the differences in theory about the charge of theft between the prosecution and defense to be found in each side's opening statements on the following points:
   a) the theft of information as opposed to the physical documents.
   b) the giving or taking of classified information to transmit to another branch of government.
   c) ownership—who owns government papers and classified studies.
   d) the effect of violating one's employer's rules vs. violation of law.
   e) authorization for top government officials practice to take classified papers on which they worked with them upon leaving government service.

37

2. Does Mr. Boudin convey Daniel Ellsberg's motive and the intent of his actions clearly and unequivocally? Does Mr. Boudin admit that Daniel Ellsberg took (if not stole) the Pentagon Papers without authority to do so?

ASSIGNMENT

1. Prepare an outline of the prosecution and defense case based on their opening statements and including each side's allegations regarding the issues itemized in Question No. 1 above (a through e).
2. Assess each witness' testimony in the pages that follow. Summarize the pertinent statements that bear on the issues outlined in Question One and include in the outline above together with page reference.

The Case for the Government

The government's first witness was Frank A. Bartimo. The government sought through his testimony to establish the identity of government exhibits and security clearance requirements as well as establish that the Pentagon Papers study was considered U. S. government property.

FRANK A. BARTIMO, SWORN

DIRECT EXAMINATION

Q (BY MR. NISSEN)   By whom are you employed, sir?

A   I am employed in the Department of Defense, Office of the Secretary of Defense.

Q   What is your title or position, sir?

A   I am the assistant general counsel for Manpower and Reserve Affairs, Health and Environment.

Q   Where are your offices located?

A   They are located in the Pentagon in Washington, D. C.

MR. NISSEN: Your Honor, may the witness have placed before him the exhibits marked for identification 1 through 20? They are all in one box, and they are all the covered volumes.

THE COURT: Yes, he may.

(Whereupon Government's Exhibits 1 through 20 were placed before the witness.)*

BY MR. NISSEN:

Q   Mr. Bartimo, have you previously examined the documents in that box?

A   I have.

Q   Prior to this trial have you been custodian in the Pentagon of those documents, Exhibits 1 through 20?

A   Yes, I have, sir.

Q   From whom were they obtained, sir?

A   These particular documents were obtained from Rand, Santa Monica, California.

Q   Have they been in government custody since they were so obtained from Rand?

A   Yes, sir.

MR. NISSEN: Your Honor, may the witness have placed before him Exhibit 24? It is a black notebook, I believe.

THE COURT: Yes.

(Whereupon Government's Exhibit 24 was placed before the witness.)

Q   Will you open the notebook, sir, and examine the contents.

Are those the Industrial Security Manuals of the Defense Department which were in effect during the period of this indictment, namely, March 3, '69, through September 30, 1970?

A   They are.

MR. NISSEN: May the witness have placed before him, your Honor, Exhibit 50?

THE COURT: Let me take a look at it.

(Brief pause.)

_____

* These consist of the 18 volumes of the Pentagon Papers study plus the Wheeler and Gurtov documents.

(Whereupon Government's Exhibit 50 was placed before the witness.) . . .

Q   Do you recognize that, sir, as a Department of Defense directive in effect during the same period that I mentioned to you in my previous question?

A   I do.

Q   Now, sir, are Department of Defense records of security clearances and security clearance terminations within the jurisdiction of your office?

A   They are, sir.

Q   Have you caused a search of those Department of Defense records to be made to determine whether Vu Van Thai and Linda Sinay had security clearances during the period March, '69 through September, '70, or at any time?

A   Yes.

Q   What did the search reveal, sir?

A   No security clearance.

MR. NISSEN: We have no further questions of this witness.

CROSS EXAMINATION

BY MR. WEINGLASS:

Q   Were you the individual who received the documents from Rand?

A   They were delivered to me, and I was a representative of the Department of Defense who received them . . .

Q   Did you instruct people to get the documents?

A   I was involved in telephoning, heard telephone calls, people being instructed to go to Rand, California, to pick up the documents, yes.

41

Q   Mr. Bartimo, were you also involved in any conversations with Mr. Warnke, Mr. Halperin, or Mr. Gelb relevant to the release of these documents to the Department of Defense?

A   I was not. . . .

Q   Do you know whether or not anyone within the Department spoke to these three gentlemen before the documents were picked up? . . .

A   I do not. No. . . .

Q   You have no knowledge, Mr. Bartimo, of how Rand got these documents?

A   Personal knowledge?

Q   Personal knowledge.

A   Well, I heard how they got to Rand, but—

Q   Not whether you have heard; I'm sorry, but personal knowledge.

A   Personal knowledge, no.

Q   Do you know how Rand got these documents?

A   No. . . .

The Government's next witness was General William DePuy. General DePuy's testimony was offered to show that one of the three sets of documents allegedly stolen, the Wheeler Report, was made by the government, at the government's expense and contained military information relative to the conduct of the war in Vietnam.

WILLIAM EUGENE DePUY, SWORN

DIRECT EXAMINATION

BY MR. NISSEN:

Q   What is your profession, sir?

A   I am an army officer.

42

Q   What is your present position in the army?

A   I am a lieutenant general. I am assigned to the Army staff. The name of my position is: I am the Assistant to the Vice-Chief of Staff of the Army.

Q   How long have you served in the Army, sir?

A   Approximately thirty-two years. . . .

In 1963 and 1962—in 1962 and '3, I served in the Pentagon on the Army staff; in 1964 I went to Vietnam and served for approximately two years as the Operations Officer in the headquarters in Saigon; in 1966 and the early part of 1967 I was the Commander of the First Infantry Division in Vietnam.

In 19— the remainder of '67 and '68 I was the Special Assistant to the Chairman of the Joint Chiefs of Staff for, what they called, counterinsurgency and special activities, and since the first of January, 1969, I have held my current job. . . .

Q   Thank you. Turning your attention back to February of 1968, sir, did you have occasion to accompany General Wheeler to South Vietnam?

A   I did.

Q   What was General Wheeler's position at that time, sir?

A   He was the Chairman of the Joint Chiefs of Staff.

Q   And you were in the position, as you said, of his Special Assistant?

A   That is correct. . . .

Q   What was the mission to which the Wheeler party was assigned, sir?

A   Well, the party was assigned to help him, and his job was to go to Vietnam, talk to the commander — commanders there, and determine the situation in the aftermath of the so-called Tet offensive, which took place in February, early February.

43

Q   And was a report of that mission submitted by General Wheeler, sir?

A   He submitted a report to the Secretary of Defense and to the President.

MR. NISSEN: May the witness be handed Government's Exhibit 19, your Honor. . . .

Q   Would you examine Exhibit 19, sir? I believe it consists of eight pages.*

A   Yes.

Q   Do you recognize that material, sir?

A   I recognize these as pages from the Wheeler Report.

Q   Did you participate in the preparation of the Wheeler Report, sir?

A   Yes, I did.

Q   Now from what source did the information in that report come?

A   . . . It came from briefings which were given to General Wheeler and all of us with him in Saigon, at General Westmoreland's headquarters; conversations with him; conversations with some of his senior commanders; for example, General Cushman, the Marine Commander in Da Nang, and General Weyand, the Commander at Bien Hoa; and their staffs.

From all the sources that I mentioned, and their staffs.

Q   You mentioned headquarters MACV. Would you tell the Court what MACV is, sir?

A   Yes. I apologize.

The senior headquarters in Vietnam is called the Military Assistance Command, Vietnam. That is the headquarters which was commanded by and served the Senior

---

* See pages 615–621 of *The Pentagon Papers*, Bantam Books (1971) for text. The Wheeler Report is one of the sets of documents which Ellsberg allegedly stole from RAND along with the Pentagon Papers study.

Military Commander, first General Westmoreland and then General Abrams, now General Weyand.

      Q   Is the document, or was the Wheeler Report, classified, sir?

      A   It was classified Top Secret.

      Q   Who made the ultimate decision on the classification to be given to the report?

      A   General Wheeler.

      Q   What was the travel cost of the Wheeler party to and from the South Vietnam area, sir?

      A   I can tell you very precisely. The Air Force charge is $615 a flying hour. It was eighteen hours out, which is $11,000, roughly speaking, and approximately the same coming back.

(8489–8498)

      The next government witness to present testimony on the charge of theft was Richard H. Best who was Rand's security officer. Mr. Best testified regarding Daniel Ellsberg's security agreements with Rand respecting the use and handling of top secret documents.

RICHARD H. BEST, SWORN

DIRECT EXAMINATION

BY MR. NISSEN:

      Q   Would you state your position and title, sir.

      A   I am the security officer of the Rand Corporation.

      Q   And how long have you been an employee of the Rand Corporation, sir?

45

A   I have been employed by the Rand Corporation since it was formed in November of 1948.

Q   During that period of time to the present —from '48 to the present, have you become familiar with the rules and regulations with regard to handling of classified materials?

A   I have.

Q   Would you briefly describe for us, please, the duties that you have as security officer and how long you have held that particular position at Rand?

A   I have been security officer of the Rand Corporation since July of 1953.

The duties are to take the regulations furnished us concerning security, which is in a book called the Department of Defense Industrial Security Manual for safeguarding classified information and work those into the procedures where we can follow the regulations given to us by the Department of Defense.

Q   Would you tell us briefly, please, what the nature of the Rand Corporation's business is?

A   The Rand Corporation is a private, non-profit independent corporation, incorporated under the laws of California, whose mission is to do analytical research on problems of domestic concern and national security.

Q   Who are the customers of Rand Corporation, sir?

A   The United States Government, municipalities, state governments and those kinds of people.

(11,674)

After prolonged argument and defense objection the DOD Industrial Security Manual and the Rand Security Manual which implemented the DOD Manual at Rand was admitted into evidence. Mr. Best then introduced the following statements and agreements signed by defendant Ellsberg.

46

BY MR. NISSEN:

Q   We have got a little fuzz on the projection there. Would you read the paragraph below "Part I, Initial Security Statement." Would you read it aloud for us, please.

A   This is the one that says:

"I hereby certify that I have received a security briefing. I shall not knowingly and willfully communicate, deliver or transmit, in any manner, classified information to an unauthorized person or agency. I am informed that such improper disclosure may be punishable under Federal Criminal Statutes. I have been instructed in the importance of classified information, and in the procedures governing its safeguarding. I am informed that willful violation or disregard of security regulations may cause the loss of my security clearance. I have read, or have had read to me, the portions of the Espionage Laws and other Federal criminal statutes relating to the safeguarding of classified information, reproduced in Appendix VI, Department of Defense Industrial Security Manual. I will report to the Federal Bureau of Investigation and to my employer, without delay, any incident which I believe to constitute an attempt to solicit classified information by an unauthorized person."

Q   And would you tell us who are the persons' signatures who appear at the bottom?

A   The signature of the employee, signing for this Initial Security Briefing, is Daniel Ellsberg, Daniel E.—Daniel Ellsberg. . . .

Q   Because of the poor quality on some of that reproduction, sir, would you read to us the lead-in paragraph and the first two paragraphs that appear in that document.

A

"I, Daniel Ellsberg, in consideration of my employment by, or professional services agreement with, the Rand Corporation, make the following statement with the understanding and intent that my statement will be used by Rand in carrying out its obligation to protect the security of Restricted Data and other classified defense information and to safeguard Privileged Information," which is asterisked and defined below.

The first one:

"1. I understand that it is the policy of the government of the United States to control the dissemination of Restricted Data and other classified defense information in such a manner as to assure the common defense and security. . . .

"2. I will not reveal to any person any Restricted Data, or classified defense information, of which I gain knowledge as a result of my employment, except in accordance with official instructions or rules of the Atomic Energy Commission, or the Department of Defense, or except as may be authorized thereafter by officials empowered to grant such authority. I understand that it is my responsibility to determine whether a prospective recipient of classified information is an authorized recipient, and that in making a disclosure of classified information to an authorized person to advise him of a classification of the information disclosed."

"4. I understand, (a) that the safeguarding of classified information is a continuing individual responsibility, (b) that the Espionage Act, Title 18 U.S.C., Sections 792, 793, 794, 795, 797, and 798, prescribe penalties for disclosure to unauthorized persons of information respecting the national defense, and for loss, destruction, or compromise of such information through gross negligence, and (c) that the provisions of the Atomic Energy Act of 1954 prescribes penalties for the disclosure of Restricted Data to unauthorized persons. I further understand that willful or gross carelessness in revealing or disclosing to any unauthorized person or in handling Restricted Data or classified defense information in violation of Department of Defense regulations and contractual obligations, and that such disclosure or disclosure of privileged information will constitute cause for termination of my employment by Rand."

THE COURT: Excuse me. Before you turn from that document, ladies and gentlemen of the jury, the introduction of this exhibit and exhibits similar to it go to the issue of knowledge, which I will explain to you at greater detail.

You are not to infer, because it would be improper and incorrect for you to infer, that any statements of law, as to what is or is not a crime or what is or is not a federal criminal offense, these documents are not admitted for the truth of those matters. . . .

(11,799–11,808)

Q   Did Linda Sinay ever work for Rand or have a security clearance there?

A   She never worked for the Rand Corporation nor had a security clearance at Rand.

Q   Subsequent to the termination of Mr. Russo's consultantship with Rand, did he ever have duties at Rand Corporation requiring any access to classified material?

A   He did not.

THE COURT: What is the date of that termination?

THE WITNESS: 8–29–69, sir. . . .

BY THE WITNESS:

A "I have requested and been granted custody of the following OSD Task Force documents. Daniel Ellsberg."

BY MR. NISSEN:

Q And OSD refers to?

A Office of the Secretary of Defense.

Q The documents are those five listed below, sir?

A That is correct.

Q And if you could raise that up again, I think it is plain, but would you read the typed sentence above the signature, sir.

A "I certify that I will retain the above documents in my custody until returned to storage and that l will not reproduce or alter any part or parts thereof."

Q Do you recognize the signature of the person that appears on that document?

A I do.

Q And it is the signature of whom?

A That is the signature of Daniel Ellsberg.

Q And would you give us the date as you can read it from your original document.

A 3 March 1969. . . .

(11,849–11,852)

(Much of Mr. Best's lengthy testimony concerned procedures for logging in and checking out classified documents according to the procedures specified in the Rand Security Manual.)

CROSS EXAMINATION

BY MR. BOUDIN:

Q   When Chief Fox delivered Exhibits 1 through 18* to Mr. Archer, they were not entered into the Top Secret Register, were they?

A   Not to my knowledge.

Q   That was not consistent with Rand's Security Manual, was it?

A   That was not consistent.

Q   Right. When they reached Mr. Archer in those boxes, they were not given a control number, were they?

A   Not to my knowledge.

Q   That is not consistent with the manual?

A   No.

Q   When they reached Mr. Archer they were not given a cover sheet, were they?

A   Not to my knowledge.

Q   That is not consistent with the manual, is it?

A   No.

THE COURT: Again, on these occasions you are referring to the Rand manual?

MR. BOUDIN: Yes, your Honor. Thank you. . . .

THE WITNESS: They were given proper storage. They were not, to my knowledge, entered on a Top Secret incoming control log, nor had a cover sheet attached.

BY MR. BOUDIN:

Q   So that the only way in which they were

---

* These are the 18 volumes of the Pentagon Papers study introduced in evidence by the government earlier.

handled in accordance with Rand Manual was that they were given proper storage, is that correct?

A   To the best of my knowledge. . . .

(12,331–12,333)

Q   When documents, classified documents are received at Rand under the Industrial Security Manual, the standard practice of Rand under the Rand Security Manual is to keep such records; is it not?

A   Yes.

Q   Now, when Volumes 1 through 18, Government's Exhibits 1 through 18, were received at Rand Washington in January, '69, what contract with the Department of Defense, if any, were they assigned to?

A   Was there a time period on that?

Q   January, '69, when they were received at Rand.

A   None to my knowledge.

(12,388–12,389)

The government's next witness was Richard A. Moorsteen, a Rand consultant who along with Dr. Ellsberg was given access to the Pentagon Papers study. Moorsteen testified that Daniel Ellsberg had brought most of the Pentagon Papers volumes to him at his office in May, 1970. Ellsberg was leaving Rand and asked Moorsteen if he wanted to have the study. Moorsteen said he called Harry Rowen, the President of Rand, for instructions as to what to do with the volumes. Within an hour,he said Ms. Jan Butler, a Top Secret Control Officer, came into his office and picked up the volumes. Jan Butler followed Moorsteen to the witness stand.

JAN BUTLER, SWORN

DIRECT EXAMINATION

BY MR. NISSEN:

Q   Where are you employed, Miss Butler?

A   At the Rand Corporation.

Q   And have you ever, while employed at the Rand Corporation, held a position of Top Secret Control Officer?

A   Yes, sir, I have.

Q   During what period of time, ma'am?

A   Approximately twelve years, between late 1958 and late 1971.

Q   Would you describe for us briefly what your duties were as Top Secret Control Officer?

A   Well, it was my job mainly to receive and process and file and distribute Top Secret materials. . . .

Q   And would you explain, please, why the eighteen exhibits, 1 through 18, were not logged in between May 20 and December 31.

A   Well, I don't have a real answer for that except that we were very busy during that time and I don't remember exactly whether—they were stored properly and awaiting my—you know, when I had time to log them in and that didn't come until later.

Q   Did anyone check them out or use them during the period May 20 through December 31?

A   No.

Q   By the way, with respect to those eighteen volumes, Exhibits 1 through 18, did you ever find them in defendant Ellsberg's possession during any of your semiannual inventories?

A   No, never.

(12,681–12,687)

53

CROSS EXAMINATION

BY MR. NESSON:

Q   Have you ever been employed by the United States government?

A   No, I haven't.

Q   More specifically, you were not an employee of the United States government in the years 1969 to 1970?

A   No, sir.

Q   Have you ever been an officer of the United States government?

A   No, I have not.

Q   And, more specifically, you were not an officer of the United States government in 1969 and 1970?

A   No.

Q   Has anyone ever told you that you were an officer or employee of the United States government, with specific reference to any of the statutes known as the Espionage Acts?

A   I think no. Not to my memory....

(12,703–12,704)

BY MR. YOUNG:

Q   Now, you received at the Top Secret Control Office Exhibits 1 through 18 on May the 20th, 1970; is that correct?

A   That's correct.

Q   Usually when you receive top secret documents marked top secret at the Top Secret Office you log them in immediately, don't you, or within a few days?

54

A   As soon as I can.

Q   It is highly unusual that there would be a several-month time gap between the receipt of top secret documents and logging them in, isn't it?

A   I think it's unusual, yes.

Q   Now, Exhibits 1 through 18 were stored in the Top Secret Control Office after May the 20th, 1970; isn't that correct?

A   Yes, they were.

Q   And they were not used by anybody between May the 20th and the end of December of 1971, were they?

A   No, that's true.

Q   They stayed in your office the entire time?

A   Yes, they did.

Q   In November of 1970 you conducted an inventory of all top secret documents inside the Top Secret Control Office?

A   That's correct.

Q   And the inventory did not show Exhibits 1 to 18 on it, did it?

A   No.

Q   Now, immediately after May 20 and continuing through September 30, 1971, did you at any time conduct an investigation—continuing through December 30th of 1970, did you at any time conduct an investigation as to the origins of Exhibits 1 to 18?

A   No, I did not.

Q   You never made any inquiry of Dr. Ellsberg whatsoever?

A   No, I think not.

Q   As far as you know, nobody at Rand made any inquiry at all?

A   As far as I know, no.

(12,824–12,825)

The government's next witness, Yvonne Ekman, was a neighbor of Dr. Ellsberg where he resided in Malibu, California.

YVONNE M. EKMAN, SWORN

BY MR. NISSEN:

Q   Now, I turn your attention to a weekend in October 1969. Did you on such a weekend have occasion to speak with defendant Ellsberg at his beach home in Malibu, California?

A   I did.

Q   Would you tell us, please, who was present and where you were when you spoke.

A   Well, I came to Dan Ellsberg's house in October and he was on his way out. It seemed to be in the afternoon and he had an accordian file of papers sitting over by the door and he said he was—he had to leave immediately and he was going to copy those papers. . . .

The government's next witness was Linda Sinay Resnick, one of the unindicted co-conspirators, who assisted in the Xeroxing of the Pentagon Papers study.

LINDA SINAY RESNICK, SWORN

BY MR. NISSEN:

Q   . . . . what occurred with regard to the use of your Xerox machine?

A   Dan and Tony used the Xerox machine.

Q   Did you see them?. .

A   Yes.

Q   On how many occasions did they use it?

The Pentagon Papers Trial

A   I'm not quite sure because I wasn't there all the time.

Q   How many occasions were you there when they used it?

A   At least four, maybe seven, eight. You know, I'm not clear. . . .

Q   And over what period of time did these copying sessions occur?

A   Ten days, two weeks.

Q   Can you place for us precisely in time when those ten days or two weeks occurred?

A   I can't. I thought it was after the 4th of July or I felt it was after the 4th of July, of 1969, but I'm not—I've never been sure, as you know, of exactly the date or the dates.

Q   How did the documents arrive at your office? Who brought them?

A   Dan.

Q   How did he bring them?

A   In a briefcase.

Q   Will you describe it for us, please.

A   It was shaped like that (indicating), and like this (indicating), like that black one that you—just like that, only it was beige.*. . . .

Q   Did you receive any payment for the use of your Xerox machine?

A   Yes.

Q   From whom?

A   Dan.

Q   What was the amount of payment, as you recall it? . . . .

THE COURT: Before you turn to that, what did that payment represent? Was it a cost to you?

_____

* She is pointing to the accordian file Yvonne Ekman described as being like the one she saw Daniel Ellsberg with.

THE WITNESS: Yes.

THE COURT: For the paper?

THE WITNESS: Cost, yes, paper, and whatever overage of copies on—you only get a certain amount on your Xerox, you know, for rental, and if you go over that, they charge you for overage.

THE COURT: It was a charge strictly for cost; no profit?

THE WITNESS: That is right.

(12,909–12,947)

The government's last witness, Deemer E. Hippensteel, was an FBI fingerprint expert who testified to finding fingerprints of Dr. Ellsberg, Anthony Russo, Ms. Resnick and Ellsberg's son, Robert, on the volumes of the Pentagon Papers study in evidence. Upon the conclusion of Mr. Hippensteel's testimony the government rested their case.

Questions for Analysis and Jury Deliberation

THE GOVERNMENT'S CASE

Bartimo Testimony
(Pages 39–42)

1. What is the significance of Bartimo's testimony that Vu Van Thai and Linda Sinay did not have security clearances?
2. How does Bartimo's direct testimony aid the government's contention that the United States owned the Pentagon Papers study at the time of the alleged theft and still owns the documents?
3. What is the purpose of Mr. Weinglass' cross examination of Mr. Bartimo?
4. Does Weinglass manage to discredit Bartimo's testimony concerning the government's ownership of the Pentagon Papers documents?

DePuy Testimony
(Pages 42–45)

1. Is General DePuy testifying from personal knowledge about the Wheeler Report?
2. What is the significance to the government's case that the Wheeler Report was a) classified "Top Secret" and b) written in February, 1968?

59

3. What is the significance of DePuy's testimony about the flying expense to the government of his party to and from Vietnam to the government's claim of ownership of the Pentagon Papers documents?

BEST TESTIMONY
(Pages 45–52)

1. What effect and relevance do the RAND security agreements signed by Daniel Ellsberg and read into evidence by Mr. Best have to the theft charges?
2. Does Judge Byrne's statement following the introduction of the agreements help clarify and mitigate the potentially prejudicial and confusing role of the agreements?
3. What is the significance of Best's assertion that upon Russo's termination as a consultant to RAND he had no details "requiring any access to classified material?"
4. What agreement did Ellsberg sign in relation to his being granted custody of the Pentagon Papers study (OSD Task Force documents)? How does this agreement differ from Ellsberg's employment agreements with RAND? Does the custody agreement give a clue as to the ownership of the OSD Task Force documents (Pentagon Papers study)?
5. What is the function of Mr. Boudin's and Mr. Young's cross examination of Mr. Best? Do Boudin and Young succeed in throwing doubt on the inference that the government owned the Pentagon Paper documents while they were at RAND's offices in Santa Monica, California?

JAN BUTLER TESTIMONY
(Pages 53–55)

1. Is Ms. Butler's testimony concerning why she did not log in the Pentagon Papers study between May 20 and December 31, 1969, after Ellsberg left the study with Moorsteen upon leaving RAND convincing?

2. Why is Mr. Nesson trying to establish in his cross examination of Ms. Butler that she has never been a federal employee?
3. Does Mr. Nesson succeed in raising doubts about the government's claim of ownership and control of the documents?
4. What is the significance of Ms. Butler not having logged in Daniel Ellsberg's volumes of the Pentagon Papers study for more than six months after Ellsberg left RAND?

YVONNE EKMAN TESTIMONY
(Page 56)

1. What is the significance of Ms. Ekman's testimony concerning what Ellsberg told her at his home in Malibu, California?
2. Is it a reasonable inference that the "accordian file of papers" contained some of the Pentagon Papers study?

LINDA SINAY RESNICK TESTIMONY
(Pages 56–58)

1, What is the significance of Sinay's testimony that Ellsberg reimbursed her only for her actual duplicating cost?

ASSIGNMENT

1. Summarize the testimony presented by the government witnesses for inclusion in your outline.

The Case for the Defense

OPENING STATEMENT ON BEHALF OF
DEFENDANT RUSSO

BY MR. WEINGLASS:

Your Honor, ladies and gentlemen of the jury, counsel, as the Court has already indicated to you, the Defendant Russo, with the Court's permission, has elected to reserve his opening until this time; that is, until the government has rested its case and the defense is about to present evidence in its own behalf.

Under the rules governing this court, I am not permitted to and I will not comment upon the government's case. That comes at the close of the case, when all counsel will review for you the evidence presented by both sides.

At this particular time I am permitted only to reveal to you the general nature and the overview of the case which the defense will present in its own behalf.

The defense will present evidence not to convince you that a crime has been committed but which should be excused by you because you agree with either the motives or the purpose of the defendants; our case, rather, will be that no violation of law has occurred.

We stand by the federal statute, as written by Congress.* The evidence in this case will show, rather, that the

---

* This refers to the espionage charges.

62

government, in bringing this prosecution, is attempting to bend and distort the laws to cover a series of acts for which there are no criminal penalties, but which they do not agree with. . . .

First, with respect to my client, Anthony Russo, he is charged now in just three counts of the thirteen-count indictment.

Briefly put, he is charged with one violation of the federal laws on theft; he is charged with one violation of the federal laws of espionage; he is charged with one violation of the federal laws respecting conspiracy. . . .

Under the theft charge, he is charged with receiving stolen goods with an intent to convert them to his own use, knowing at the time he received them that they were, in fact, stolen.

So as we look at the two charges under espionage and theft, we will see that my client, Mr. Russo, is charged with being a receiver under "theft," and a person who willfully retains under "espionage." Nowhere in this indictment is he charged with giving these documents to anyone, with conveying them, or transmitting them. The sole basis of the government's case against Mr. Russo is that he had contact with these documents as a receiver of them and as a person who willfully retained them.

Although this indictment charges acts over a lengthy period of time, some nineteen months in all, March 1st, 1969, to September 30, 1970, the evidence we will offer will conform almost precisely to the evidence offered by the government already respecting my client's contact with the volumes.

That contact, you will recall, was testified to by Miss Sinay, now Mrs. Resnick, when she said in, over this nineteen-month period of time, which is the time covered by the indictment, that just a brief period of some two weeks, or four or seven or eight occasions, she saw the defendant Russo come in contact with these volumes on those few occasions in the evening at her advertising agency here in Los Angeles.

She said that his contact consisted very much the same as hers, a physical touching, as witnessed by the fingerprints, of the documents in the course of assisting Daniel Ellsberg in the Xeroxing.

The defendant Russo did not bring the documents to the advertising agency; the defendant Russo did not leave with the documents from the advertising agency.

In the course of his being in the advertising agency those few hours, he was never alone with the documents; he never had them in his own custody without Daniel Ellsberg being present; he never had them in his control; they were never under his, in contemplation of law, as it will be explained by the Court, under his dominion.

In short, the government has failed, and our case will support that failure, to show that the defendant Russo, in contemplation of law, received or willfully retained. . . .

Moving on to the theft counts, the defendants will show two things with respect to the theft counts. First, they will show that there is a reasonable doubt as to who in fact were the owners of these documents in 1969. Secondly, they will show that the documents were not in fact stolen or converted by the defendants.

The Court will instruct you at the end of the case that in order for the United States government to prevail in this case, he must convince you beyond a reasonable doubt that the materials we are talking about were the property of the United States, also must convince you beyond a reasonable doubt that the materials were, in fact, stolen or converted.

With respect to the eighteen volumes that constitute the Pentagon Papers, the evidence will show that all the persons who treated the documents during this particular period of time—the United States government, the three gentlemen whom you have heard so much about already, Mr. Warnke, Dr. Gelb, and Dr. Halperin, and the Rand Corporation—all treated these documents in a consistent way and in a way which indicated that they were not the property of the United States.

It goes without saying that the materials were generated by the government; it goes without saying that the government's name is on the documents; it also goes without saying that the documents were marked and stamped "Top Secret," but we will offer to you testimony from expert persons who have great familiarity with this procedure, and they will tell you that it is a frequent practice of government—even a common practice of government for persons who served the government, upon the termination of that service, to take with them as their private papers copies of the materials which were produced in the course of their service to the government.

The government of the United States recognized this fact in 1969, and, by appropriate tax regulations, allows these persons who leave the government to contribute these very documents to archives and libraries in the country. . . .

These documents, the nineteen volumes, were not the original copies of the materials that were produced. As they state on their cover, they are a copy themselves, a Xerox copy. I think it is copy 1 of five copies, and that designation appears on each of the blue covers, with one exception, and I believe it refers to it as being copy 1 of four copies.

We will call to the witness stand Dr. Halperin. He will tell you that in 1969, in the early part of that year, himself, Dr. Gelb, and Mr. Warnke were, all officials of the government, actively employed and working in an office of the State Assistant Secretary of Defense for International Security Affairs.

In the early part of 1969, as the Johnson administration was coming to a close and the Nixon administration was coming in, they were planning to leave government service, and so, together, with a number of other employees who did the same, they, gathered together a number of documents and papers upon which they had worked, and they crated their documents and papers into five boxes, and in those five boxes were thirty-eight volumes of the Pentagon study, eighteen of which are included in the government's case here.

These volumes were sent to Rand Corporation in Washington, D. C., and they were received by the Rand Corporation on January 21, 1969. The documents were sent to the Rand Corporation, not pursuant to any contract or agreement between the Department of Defense and the particular office in which they worked and the Rand Corporation, but as a result of a private agreement which had been worked out and reduced to writing on December 18, 1968. You have already seen that agreement on the screen signed by Warnke, Gelb, and Halperin.

They were sent by these three gentlemen for the purpose of being stored in the Rand Corporation facility in Washington, D. C. They were received by the Rand Corporation for that identical purpose. There was no intention on the part of Rand or on the part of these three gentlemen—and, indeed, there was the opposite intention, that these documents should become part of the inventory of the Rand Corporation and to be circulated generally amongst its employees for work on government contracts.

The documents were received by Rand. The evidence will show they were not logged in; the evidence will show there were no IBM cards that were set up for them; there was no pink sheet placed on their cover, that top secret access sheet that you heard Mr. Best refer to; they were not monitored; they were not put in the system of circulation.

Instead, they were treated by Rand precisely as the three individuals had agreed with Rand they should be treated. They were put in drawer 82 and drawer 81 for storage.

No one in Rand, under the agreement of December 18, 1968, could have gained access to those volumes, no matter how urgent his need was, no matter how urgent his work was, without the express permission of the three individuals who sent those documents in the waning days of their employment in the Pentagon to the Rand Corporation for storage.

Our evidence will show that even as late as June of 1971, that these volumes could not be returned to the United States government by the Rand Corporation without the express approval of Warnke, Gelb, and Halperin, even though by June of 1971 all three were no longer in the government service and were, in fact, private individuals.

Finally, our evidence will show that the remainder of those five cases of materials that were sent by these three gentlemen to Rand for storage, exclusive of the other twenty volumes of the Pentagon Papers that stayed there, were donated by these three men to the archives of the United States as a private donation by them.

So as you look at the course of the documents and as you look at the way they were treated by Warnke, Gelb, and Halperin, the officials of Rand, the persons in Rand responsible for them, and, indeed, by the United States government itself, it is clear that it has not been established beyond a reasonable doubt as to who, in fact, the owners of the eighteen volumes were during the period of time named in the indictment.

But even if the volumes were the property of the United States government, we will prove to you that these volumes were neither stolen nor converted by the defendant Ellsberg, nor received as stolen property by the defendant Russo.

Our evidence will show the following: In March of 1969 and again in August of 1970 the defendant Ellsberg, with the knowledge of Warnke, Gelb and Halperin, and with the approval of the President of the Rand Corporation, Mr. Rowen, obtained these documents where they were stored in Rand in Washington, D. C. He did not obtain them for any illegal purpose, and, as a matter of fact, no illegal purpose is alleged.

He obtained them because he was working at the

Rand Corporation at that time on a project that would have been assisted by his reading them, and he knew Dr. Gelb, having worked under him and doing work on the Pentagon Papers study the year before, and Dr. Gelb had agreed in return for Dr. Ellsberg's services on the Pentagon Papers study that he would have access if and when he wanted to Dr. Gelb's copy of the study.

So he was given authority to take the volumes and to take them back to the Rand Corporation in Santa Monica.

He brought them back to Rand Santa Monica, the evidence will show, and he placed them with the knowledge of the President of the Rand Corporation again in his top secret safe, which is maintained in his office at the Santa Monica facility.

They were not placed in the top secret control system; they were not given to Jan Butler; they were not given to Mr. Best.

The evidence will show the reason they were not given to these individuals was because Dr. Ellsberg, before he left Washington, D. C., was instructed by the Vice President of the Rand Corporation in Washington, Mr. Henderson, who will appear and testify, not to place them in the top secret control system at Rand in Santa Monica because, under agreement of December 18, 1968, the agreement I referred to, the three individuals, Warnke, Gelb and Halperin, were entitled to have access within 72 hours, and that is the last paragraph of that agreement, whenever they deemed that access in their interest was necessary.

If they would be placed in the top secret control system in Rand Santa Monica, Mr. Henderson felt Rand would have been in violation of its understanding with those three private individuals.

So Dr. Ellsberg was instructed not to place them in the system, and he placed them instead in his top secret safe and he placed them in his safe pursuant to that instruction by the Vice President of Rand and with the knowledge again of the President of Rand, Mr. Rowen.

During all the time that the documents resided in his top secret safe, Rand had a record and knowledge of where they were. The three individuals who sent the documents to Rand had a record and knowledge of where they were. At all times they were held available to both Rand, and you will recall Dr. Moorsteen, and they were held available to Warnke, Gelb and Halperin, precisely in accordance with the private understanding of December 18, 1968.

The documents remained in the safe. They were never at the home of Dr. Ellsberg overnight. It is true they were temporarily removed and Xeroxed on those few occasions referred to by Mrs. Resnick, but they were always returned to the Rand facility before the work day the following day.

While no one here claims that there was authority to remove the documents from the building or that there was express authority for Xeroxing, and no one here claims that they may or may not have violated the rules of their employer, nor is there any proof that there was an intent, on the part of Dr. Ellsberg or Anthony Russo to substantially deprive the owners of these documents of the documents, to remove the documents permanently from their possession, or to alter the documents in terms of their appearance or their makeup.

You will be instructed at the end of the case with respect to what constitutes theft under law,* but our evidence will show you that there was no intent to permanently remove, no intent to substantially deprive, and in fact no alteration or loss of the documents to the owners.

You will recall that at the beginning of this case you were questioned as to whether or not you could separate a violation of an employer's rules from an alleged infraction of a federal statute. Although there might have been an infraction

---

* This is the judge's function in charging the jury.

of the employer's rules, an infraction for which these defendants will pay the rest of their lives because they are not employable in their chosen profession—

THE COURT: Just the facts of the case.

MR. WEINGLASS: —there has not been a violation of federal law in a sense of a substantial deprivation or a harm to the owner of the documents.

Furthermore, on those documents when my client held those documents in his hand, he was not a receiver, as the Court will define that term for you at the end of the case. He never had custody or control of the documents; nor did he know or have reason to believe that the documents were stolen or would be stolen; nor did he convert the documents to his own use. . . .

This is not simply a case of documents; this is a case of documents and two men, the defendants Ellsberg and Russo.

I cannot speak for the defendant Ellsberg with respect to this, but I can inform you at this time that the defendant Russo will take the stand as a witness and will offer testimony in his own behalf. He will tell you of his background, such as Mr. Boudin outlined in his opening, of how he came to the Rand Corporation, how he, in those fretful years of the early sixties, offered his talents through Rand to the government, and how he came to realize—and completed his education in Vietnam—slowly came to the realization that what the government needed was not only the talents of the young men, but its courage as well.

He will tell you how he came on those evenings in question to assist Daniel Ellsberg in the copying of these documents in order to get them to Congress. He will also candidly acknowledge, as you must now readily see for yourselves, that he was misbriefed in the Rand Corporation into believing that it was a federal crime to copy a classified document and, thereby, thought wrongfully that his action in copying the documents

70

constituted a violation of federal law, but it would be an injustice to my client for you to consider his own beliefs, his own subjective beliefs as a result of having been misinformed by the security briefing process of Rand, that he was committing a crime when, in fact, and under the instructions of law given to you by the Court, he had not committed an offense or violated the law of the United States. . . .

We offer our case to you in its whole form, and we hope that at the end of the case you will find that, not only is there not a reasonable doubt with respect to these charges, but, by the overwhelming evidence, these materials could not have been either materials that were subject to an application of the espionage laws or materials that were, in fact, stolen, being the property of the United States.

Thank you.

THE COURT: Thank you, Mr. Weinglass.

(13,546–13,604)

The first defense witness to give testimony relative to the theft count in the indictment was Morton H. Halperin, a senior fellow at the Brookings Institution and former Deputy Assistant Secretary of Defense for International Security Affairs (ISA). At the time of his testimony, Halperin was a full-time consultant to the defense.

MORTON H. HALPERIN, SWORN

DIRECT EXAMINATION

BY MR. NESSON:

Q Turning your attention now to your period of your employment in the ISA, did you have any responsibilities in connection with the Pentagon Papers, the production of the so-called Pentagon Papers?

A Yes, I did.

Q What were those responsibilities?

A Well, my responsibilities was for general supervision of the task force which produced the Pentagon Papers.

Q Now, are you, then, familiar with the production of those papers?

A Yes, I am.

Q Now, will you please describe to the jury step by step how the task force report or the Pentagon Papers, or whatever you wish to call it, were produced.

A Well, the first contact I had with it occurred sometime in June of 1967. I was called by a man who was then my boss, Assistant Secretary of Defense John McNaughton, to his office.

When I came in there was also present then Colonel, now General, Robert Gard, who was the—one of the two military assistants to the Secretary of Defense Robert McNamara.

Colonel Gard indicated to me and to Mr. McNaughton that Secretary of Defense McNamara wanted a study done which would be a history of the involvement of the United States in Vietnam, that he wanted this study to be encyclopedic and objective and that he had prepared, and Colonel Gard had with him, a long list of questions which were among the questions that Colonel Gard said that Mr. McNamara wanted answered as part of his history of where we were and how we had gotten where we were in Vietnam.

We then had a discussion among the three of us as to how this study might best be done. We agreed that it would have to be done in the immediate office of the Secretary; that is, not in one of the offices of the Assistant Secretaries, and that it would have to be done by a full time staff which would work intensely on the study. At that time our estimates were that the job could be done in perhaps three or four months.

And as a result of this meeting, Colonel Gard prepared a memorandum to the Secretary of Defense recommending that a full time task force of perhaps six or eight people be set up in the immediate office of the Secretary of Defense to prepare the study. The recommendation was that I be the full time director of the task force.

(16,766–16,769)

BY MR. NESSON:

Q When you say that the designation "Sensitive" was applied to the documents so that their existence—indicating that their existence should be kept from other Americans, what other Americans are you referring to?

A In this case it included, as I say, everybody who was not directly involved either in the writing of the study or in supplying documentation for the studies.

Q Who would that include?

A That would include officials of the Department of Defense, of the Department of State, of the White House, of the U. S. Military Assistance Command, Vietnam, members of Congress, and the public in general.

Q Were there some considerations which you had in mind in coming to your decision that these documents should be marked "Sensitive"?

Did you receive any instructions with reference to these studies and their markings?

THE WITNESS: I received instructions that the existence of the study was not to be revealed except to people who had to have it.

THE COURT: From whom did you receive those instructions?

THE WITNESS: From the military assistant to the Secretary, indicating those were his instructions.

THE COURT: What was his name?

THE WITNESS: The Secretary of Defense was

73

Robert McNamara; the military assistant was Colonel Gard.
(16,798–16,810)

BY MR. NESSON:

Q   And did you have occasion in January, 1969, to have any conversations with others in the Department of Defense with respect to the sending of a copy of the task force report to the Rand Corporation?

A   The conversation may have been in December, but they were either in December or January I had such conversations.

Q   With whom did you have these conversations?

A   With Paul Warnke and Leslie Gelb.

Q   And what were the circumstances which led to your having these conversations?

A   We were all planning to leave, or expected to be leaving, the Department of Defense, and the question arose as to whether there were any papers or documents which we should take with us in the sense that we would pack them up and have shipped for us to some place where we would store them.

Q   And what was the occasion for your all leaving the Department of Defense?

A   This was the end of the Johnson administration, and we were all appointed in positions which were not protected by the Civil Service, or at least I was and Mr. Warnke was, and the expectation was that all three of us would be leaving when the new administration came in.

Q   Was there any practice with which you were familiar at that time of officials in the Executive Branch, particularly in the Pentagon, packing up their papers, as you say, at the point of changeover of the administration?

MR. NISSEN: Objection. Immaterial.

THE COURT: Sustained.

74

BY MR. NESSON:

Q Following those conversations, Mr. Halperin, what did you do with respect to the copy 1 of the task force report?

A Following the first conversation that I had with Mr. Warnke and Mr. Gelb, I phoned Harry Rowen, the president of the Rand Corporation.

Q What was the purpose of your telephone conversation with Mr. Rowen?

A The purpose of the conversation was to find out whether these documents and a number of other documents could be stored at the Rand Corporation for myself and Warnke and Gelb.

Q Did you, in that conversation, come to an agreement with Mr. Rowen as to the terms and conditions under which the papers would be stored at the Rand Corporation?

A Yes, I did. . . .

THE COURT: Well, when was the conversation? Where were you when it took place, and who is Mr. Rowen?

THE WITNESS: I was in my office in the Pentagon. The conversation was either late in December of 1968 or early in January of 1969. Mr. Rowen was at that time the president of the Rand Corporation.

BY MR. NESSON:

Q What were the terms of the arrangement which you worked out with Mr. Rowen as a result of that telephone conversation?

A The understanding was that we would put together a set of materials that we wished to have stored for us at the Rand Corporation, that Rand would store these materials in a top secret safe in a room which was authorized to have such a safe, that the material would be available to us at our request, and that the material would not be treated by Rand the way it treated materials which came to it under contract, but rather would be stored outside the normal Rand top secret control system, but simply put in a separate top secret safe.

Q When you refer to materials, what materials specifically are you referring to?

A Well, the materials that were gathered together with the volumes of the task force, the Vietnam task force, the Pentagon Papers, which were then typed in final form. That was apparently thirty-seven separate studies, two copies of one study—apparently by mistake included—an additional set of notebooks, which were those of John McNaughton, which had remained when he had been killed, which were the McNaughton private papers, and then there were some additional notebooks which were materials that had either been written by Mr. Warnke or by me or by Mr. Gelb during the course of our work in the Pentagon, and we—which we wished to store along with these other materials.

MR. NESSON: Mr. Bennion, could you project B-1.

(Slide shown.)

Q Now, does B-1 embody the arrangement which you worked out by telephone with Mr. Rowen?

A It embodies the basic elements of it; not all of the details of it.

Q Now, would you describe for the jury what details are not embodied in that argreement.

A It does not embody the specific understanding that these documents would not be included in the Rand top secret control system or given to the Rand top secret control officers, but rather would be kept under the immediate control of either Mr. Rowen or Mr. Henderson, who was the Vice President of the Rand Washington office. Apart from that, I think it covered the essential elements.

Q Now, with respect to the arrangement that the material should be kept in the control of Mr. Henderson or —was there another party that you mentioned there?

A Mr. Rowen.

Q With respect to the term of the arrangement, as you just described it, what was the purpose of that term?

A The purpose of the arrangement was to insure, on the one hand, that the three people who signed the agreement—Mr. Warnke, Mr. Gelb, and myself—could get access to the documents, as it says in the memorandum, on our own authority, which might have been a problem if the documents was in the formal Rand top secret control system, which would require the Rand top secret control officer or the security officer of the Rand Corporation to specify that we had a need to know —to see these documents in connection with Rand projects.

We also felt that the document should not get wide distribution within the Rand Corporation, which is why the document spelled out rather precisely the procedures under which people at Rand might get access. And again we felt that if the documents—or I felt that if the documents were in the Rand top secret control system, the process of granting access might come out of our control and into the control of the Rand security officers.

And finally, the very existence of this study continued to be a closely guarded secret, even within the government, and my feeling was that if it entered the Rand top secret control system, it would then show up on Rand inventories, which were accessible to people from the Air Force and the Defense Department, which monitored the Rand Corporation, and in that way might become known to people who were not supposed to know even of the very existence of the study.

Q Did the agreement you made with Mr. Rowen incorporate the terms of the Industrial Security Manual?

A No, it did not.

BY MR. NESSON:

Q Now, directing your attention to the end of February or early March, 1969, did you receive a request from any person that Dr. Ellsberg be permitted to have access to the OSD task force materials?

77

A   Yes. I'm not sure of the precise date, but some time in that general period I did receive such a request.

Q   From whom did you receive the request?

A   I received a phone call from Mr. Harry Rowen, who was still the president of the Rand Corporation, asking me to give my approval and to secure the approval of one of the other two gentlemen named in the memorandum for Daniel Ellsberg to have access to the task force volumes.

Q   And what action was taken upon that request?

A   I consulted with Mr. Warnke and Mr. Gelb. I then called Mr. Rowen back and indicated that we would not grant approval to Mr. Ellsberg to have access to these documents.

Q   Did you receive some further request that access for Dr. Ellsberg be granted?

A   Yes. In that second phone call I received a second request from Mr. Rowen that Mr. Ellsberg be granted access to the documents.

Q   And what action was taken upon that request?

A   I then telephoned Mr. Gelb and told him that Mr. Ellsberg was working on a contract for the Department of Defense on the lessons learned from Vietnam, and that Mr. Rowen felt that Mr. Ellsberg could make good use of the OSD task force volumes in working on this Defense Department contract, and that he felt very strongly that given the fact that Rand was storing the volumes for us, we should honor this request, which was at that time the only request that he had made, and give access to the volumes to Mr. Ellsberg.

THE COURT: What was the date of this conversation?

THE WITNESS: All of these conversations took place in February, March or April of 1969.

BY MR. NESSON:

        Q And what action was taken upon that request?

        A I then called Mr. Rowen and indicated to him that Mr. Gelb and I had approved access for Dr. Ellsberg to the OSD task force volumes.

        Q Did you discuss the subject of storage conditions of the documents at the Rand Corporation?

        A Yes, we did.

        Q And could you relate the substance of that discussion?

        A I indicated to Mr. Rowen that we would agree to have Dr. Ellsberg take the documents from the Rand Washington office to the Rand Santa Monica office, provided that the documents continued to be treated as they had been in the Rand Washington office, that is, that they not be put in the custody of the top secret control officer, that they not be given Rand top secret access sheets, and, in conformity with the provision 4 of the memorandum to Mr. Rowen, that they be available in Washington on 72 hours' notice.

(16,838–16,880)

        Mr. Halperin went on to say that at the time the copies of the Pentagon Papers study were distributed those persons to whom Halperin gave copies were for the most part private citizens and not in government employment. Halperin also expressed his opinion that the study does not represent an authoritative view of the thinking of the American government as to American policy in the war in Vietnam. He based this view on the fact that the study did not have complete access to documents as he testified earlier and that what documents were used were not authoritative themselves when not confirmed by personal interviews. The volumes did not reflect the views of the Secretary of Defense; they were simply the opinions of the several writers in the task force.

79

CROSS EXAMINATION

BY MR. NISSEN:

Q Did your private papers include all documents that came to you in the course of your work?

A No, they did not.

Q Was there any document that came to you in the course of your work that, in your judgment, you could not have taken a copy of as a part of your private papers?

A Not if I had arranged to store it in a facility which had the proper storage facilities for the document as it was marked by the government.

Q So in your judgment you could have taken National Intelligence Estimates, CIA reports, State Department cables, the Wheeler report, back-channel communications, and anything else that came across your desk or to your attention?

A Yes.

May I explain my answer?

THE COURT: Yes, you may.

THE WITNESS: I have, in the course of research that I had done for the government and in the course of reading the memoirs of former government officials—and I have read, I think, virtually all of the memoirs written by former government officials—I have done one or several classified research projects for the government, and in the course of the reading I have done, I have found a number of references to the fact that people were writing their books based on papers that they had taken with them from the government.

And it was clear from the papers that they quoted, from the documents that they had quoted, that they had taken with them papers of the kind described in the question.

From the interviews that I conducted with former officials of the government for research projects that I had done, it was clear that they had taken with them materials of the kind that I had mentioned.

Also at the time that I was leaving the government I talked to a number of other officials who were planning to leave the government at the end of the Johnson administration and asked them what kind of papers they were taking and where they were sending those papers.

So, on the basis of interviews that I had conducted with people in the course of which they referred to the private papers that they had taken with them, in the course of reading that I had done in memoirs in which people in the bibliography and the appendices referred to the private papers they had taken with them, in the course of conversations that I had with people leaving the Johnson administration at the end of it and conversations that I had had with people who had previously left the Johnson administration, I concluded that the standard practice that many people followed in the government was to take with them papers that they had written and any other government documents that came to their attention within the government which they felt were a necessary part of telling the historical story which centered around their own papers.

So I concluded that, according to that common practice, that I had the right to take these papers which fit in with and were part of the story that would be told by my private papers for the deposit in a facility that had the requisite storage facilities to hold materials so marked, and with the notion that they would later be available to historians and other scholars who would be interested in the events which I had participated in the government.

BY MR. NISSEN:

Q   By whose authority did you take the classified materials which you have characterized as your private papers?

A   I did not take them; I had them shipped to a facility which was authorized to secure them. My understanding was that the law—in particular, the Presidential Papers Library Act, authorized—

THE COURT: Excuse me. Again, what the law is, I will instruct the jury on. . . .

Q   Sir, on your departure from government service did you represent to the government that you did not then have in your possession, custody, or control any document or other things containing, or incorporating, information affecting the national defense or other security information classified Top Secret, Secret, or Confidential to which you obtained access during your employment or assignment?

A   Yes, I did. But I would like to explain my answer.

THE COURT: You may.

THE WITNESS: I took those words to mean in my possession, not material that I had arranged to have deposited in a government security facility.

(17,126–17,133)

The government tried further to discredit Halperin's testimony by trying to establish that Halperin was involved along with Daniel Ellsberg in leaking the order of battle figures in the Wheeler report to the New York Times.

BY MR. NISSEN:

Q   Whether you saw that article or not, sir, at about that time, were you aware of the newspaper disclosure in an article in the New York Times under Neil Sheehan and Hedrick Smith's name?

A   Yes, this is the article and I did see it at the time.

THE COURT: Does that article refresh your recollection as to the approximate date?

THE WITNESS: It is the 10th of March, 1968.

BY MR. NISSEN:

Q Now, sir, on October 21, 1971, is it not true that you refused to answer the questions furnished you by the FBI with regard to the Wheeler report and Mr. Ellsberg?

A I saw no connection between questions about the work that was done in my office on the Wheeler report and the publication in the New York Times of the Pentagon Papers.

Q Even though the Wheeler report, the eight pages, had appeared in the New York Times in 1971, sir?

MR. NESSON: Objection as argumentative.

THE COURT: Sustained.

BY MR. NISSEN:

Q Sir, one of the questions you refused to answer on October 21, '71, was whether Mr Ellsberg was a member of the group working in your office in March of '68; isn't that correct?

A As I say, I do not remember any of the specific questions. There were a group of questions read out, all of which concerned work being done in my office in the Pentagon in March of 1968, and I believe perhaps also concerning the publication of this article, and I saw no relevance of any of those questions, and I refused to answer all of them.

As I said, I was given no explanation of the relevance of the questions.

Q On that same occasion you refused to answer the question of whether you furnished or authorized anyone to furnish the Wheeler report to Mr. Ellsberg, or any part of it; isn't that true?

A I can, if you like, repeat the same statement. I do not remember any of the specific questions that were asked: I was asked a whole series of questions about the work being done in my office in March, '68, perhaps also about the leak of this to the New York Times, and I replied that until I was furnished with an explanation of the relevance of those questions to the publication of the Pentagon Papers in the New York Times, that I would not answer those questions.

The FBI agents said that they did not know the relevance, that the questions had been simply given to them by the Defense Department, and they agreed that they would go back to the Defense Department and ask the Defense Department the relevance of the questions, and that if it was felt that answers were needed, they would either come back to me or that the Defense Department would, and I never subsequently had a request to answer the questions or an explanation of their relevance.

(17,180–17,194)

BY MR. NISSEN:

Q   Was the basis for the approval of Mr. Rowen's request the fact that Mr. Ellsberg was working on Vietnam matters for Rand under a DOD contract and because he still retained his Defense Department clearance?

A   . . .The reason for my approval was the very strong representations from Mr. Rowen, who was the person who had agreed to store this material for us, that he felt that Daniel Ellsberg should be given access to this material. . . .

Q   Was your approval of Rowen's request given reluctantly, sir?

A   No, it was not.

Q   On October 6, 1971, did you advise interviewing FBI agents that your approval was given reluctantly?

A   I have no recollection of that. I certainly told them that Mr. Gelb's approval was given reluctantly, and I may have said that approval for Mr. Ellsberg to have access was given reluctantly.

(17,204–17,206)

The defense's next witness was Lawrence J. Henderson, former Vice President of the Rand Corporation, who testified as a "fact" witness. Henderson corroborated Halperin's story that the Pentagon Papers study were received at Rand's Washington office under a private storage agreement by which only Halperin, Gelb and Warnke were entitled to grant access to the documents which were not monitored or logged into Rand's Top Secret Control System. Henderson also confirmed that Ellsberg was given authorized access to the papers.

The stage was now set for the direct testimony of Anthony Russo and Daniel Ellsberg. The defense lawyers had moved to have the court suppress all statements made by the defendants against the war before numerous public and private groups since the indictment. The prosecution had had the defendants under constant surveillance by the FBI since the indictment and the defense sought to keep the defendants' post indictment statements from being used by the government on cross examination. The motion was denied. Anthony Russo was the first to take the witness stand in the tensely expectant courtroom.

ANTHONY RUSSO, SWORN

DIRECT EXAMINATION

BY MR. WEINGLASS:

Q   Mr. Russo, where do you presently reside?
A   My residence is in Santa Monica, California.
Q   How long have you lived in Santa Monica?
A   Since the summer of '64.
Q   With whom do you reside?
A   I reside with my wife, Katherine Barkley.
Q   Are you presently employed?

A   I have been unemployed since June 18th, when the litigation—when I began to become concerned with litigation in this case.

Q   June 18th of what year?

A   June 18th of 1971. That was right after the Pentagon Papers were released and—. . .

Q   Prior to this morning, just now, have you ever had occasion to hold those ten documents* in your hands?

A   Yes, back in the fall of 1969 when I Xeroxed them.

Q   Prior to your Xeroxing them, had you seen them?

A   No.

Q   Since the occasion of their being copied, have you seen them?

A   Only here in the courtroom.

Q   When these ten documents were copied, were you alone?

A   No.

Q   Who was with you?

A   Daniel Ellsberg, Linda Sinay.

Q   Just engaged in the copying process?

A   Yes.

Q   Anybody else engaged?

A   Robert Ellsberg, Dan's son was there on occasion.

Q   Now, you refer to the fall of '69. Would you indicate how long a period of time these particular documents were copied?

A   It was a period of several weeks.

Q   On how many separate occasions?

A   My best recollection is around eight, give or take a few, around eight times.

------

* Referring to 10 volumes of the Pentagon Papers study.

Q Do you recall where they were copied?

A Yes. They were copied over a flower shop at an advertising agency at the corner of Melrose and Crescent Heights in Hollywood.

Q What time of day were they copied?

A Usually after the work day, beginning around dinnertime on into the night.

Q Was Daniel Ellsberg always present during the copying of the documents?

A Yes, he was.

Q Did you on any of those eight occasions bring the documents of the exhibits to the place where they were copied?

A No, I did not.

Q Did you on any of those eight occasions leave with the exhibits?

A No, I did not.

Q When the copying was completed?

A No. . .

Q At the time the copying was done, did you know where the exhibits came from?

A Yes. They came from Dan's safe at Rand.

Q At the time the copying was done, did you know where the exhibits went after the copying was completed?

A Yes. He would take them right directly back to the safe in his office.

Q Do you know how, sir—sorry, strike that. Did you know how at the time of the copying Daniel Ellsberg obtained these exhibits?

A I knew that they had come from Washington.

Q And did you find that out?

A After we began to copy.

Q In addition to the people you've already mentioned who were engaged in the copying, was there anyone else present at the advertising agency while the copying occurred?

A   Yes. On one night—I believe it was just one night—there was a friend named Kimberly Rosenberg there, and on another occasion there was a gentleman who is a friend of both Dan's and myself named Vu Van Thai.

Q   Was Mr. Thai there on more than one occasion?

A   He was only there once.

Q   Did Mr. Thai engage in any of the copying?

A   No, he did not. He sat in the next room.

Q   And in the course of that evening, did you see Mr. Thai do anything in connection with any of these documents?

A   I saw him holding a document case and reading it. Could I explain?

Q   Yes. Explain the circumstances of his holding the document.

A   Yes. I had been sitting in the next room talking with Mr. Thai. I was talking about research work I had done. I was talking about a paper that I had written which was about the Vietnamese war. It was about the relationship between social and economic factors and resistance in Vietnam; that is, the fighting. My papers showed that the United States was in Vietnam fighting the war against the poor people. Mr. Thai and I were discussing this. We were discussing the relationship between economic classes and the strength of resistance in Vietnam.

Mr. Thai is a very, very knowledgeable man. I found that he had read a great deal in the literature; that is, in the political science work that is done here in the United States, and I found him to be very interesting, so we chatted on and on about that and about a lot of other things. Then, at one point, Dan, who was in the next room at the Xerox machine, said, "Hey, Thai, look at this." He came into the room and said, "Thai, read that. Isn't that interesting?"

Thai took the book and read a few pages and handed it back to Dan.

Q Was that the full extent of his contact with any of these documents?

A That's the only time I ever saw him have any contact. I said to myself at the time, "My goodness, those things have top secret marks. We should be a little more careful than that," but it's very interesting, you know — you know — when you're reading something and you're a scholar—

THE COURT: Excuse me, Mr. Russo. Redirect your question.

THE WITNESS: Well, I want to explain. It will just take a minute.

THE COURT: No.

(19,074–19,082)

Russo went on at this point to describe how he came to work at Rand and his work in Vietnam while in Rand's employ.

Q Now, during the eighteen-month stay in Vietnam, do you recall what work you were doing for the Rand Corporation?

A Yes. I went to Rand—I mean, I went to Vietnam to join Rand's field operation for the Viet Cong motivation and morale project, the so-called Viet Cong Motivation and Morale Project—and I say so-called, because I don't like the name "Viet Cong." It really doesn't describe those members of the Vietnamese independence movement properly, but since it is known as that, I will call it the "Viet Cong Motivation and Morale Project."

That project was done by Rand for the Department of Defense, and there was an operation in Vietnam, a headquarters in Saigon, where several Rand people administered interviews with prisoners that were taken by the U. S. Army, by the Marines, by the Saigon Army, and my job was to administer a team of Vietnamese interviewers.

There were about four or five interviewers, and we traveled all over the country.

Q Did you yourself, in connection with your

work on the project, render any report to any of the agencies of the government?

A Yes. There was one report called—that was a research memorandum called "Some Findings of the Viet Cong Motivation and Morale Study."

I wrote one report for the Air Force that had been—at the request of the Air Force. They wanted us to take all the information out of the interviews that we had on anti-personnel weapons, so I did that. I went through all the interviews, pulled out all the information on anti-personnel weapons. We went—the interviews were quite lengthy, and a lot of times the prisoners, the refugees, the defectors would tell us about how it was to live under the bombing.

And the Air Force wanted to know what the effect of the weapons was. They were very interested in that.

So I went through all the interviews and pulled out all the information on the anti-personnel weapons. The anti-personnel weapon is a weapon which is designed to kill human beings. It is not designed to destroy property.

In Vietnam over half the tonnage that is dropped is anti-personnel weapons. The problem is, more often than not, the anti-personnel weapons fall on civilians.

I saw in the interviews many examples of young children who would pick up an anti-personnel weapon that hadn't gone off—they were very shiny sometimes, and they are very attractive to kids who happen along and don't know what they are.

So, on many occasions a kid would pick this up, take it home, show it to his parents, and then it would go off and kill the whole family. I saw many instances of this back in 1965, 1966. They were also dropped in North Vietnam. In the Rand interviews there are also examples of anti-personnel weapons being dropped in North Vietnam. So, I wrote up a report that was about 30 or 40 pages long which outlined this. I was kind of secretly hoping that when the Air Force saw how badly these things were for people who they got dropped on, that maybe they'd quit using them. But I think I was very naive because they never quit using them. They escalated using them. By now they have dropped something like six million tons of these anti-personnel weapons and they drop them at the rate of 30 pounds every time you snap your fingers.

BY MR. WEINGLASS:

Q Now, in connection with your work on the Viet Cong Motivation and Morale study, was that work cited in any of the exhibits which are before you?

A Yes, it is. It's cited in the Exhibit No. 6—no, it's not here before me. It's in Exhibit 6 which is Volume IV.A.5.

(19,097–19,102)

Q With respect to your interviews with prisoners, is there anyone in particular, any particular interview that you can recall down to this date?

A Yes. There was one particular interview that I did.

MR. NISSEN: Object to that as immaterial, your Honor, what particular interview he might have had that he can recall.

THE COURT: Overruled.

THE WITNESS: There was one particular interview that I remember to this day. I don't remember the man's name, but I remember his file number in the Rand system. His file number is AG132. This man was the strongest man I have ever met, that is, his constitution, his personality. He was the strongest man I have ever met in my life. It had quite an effect on me because it was in the spring of 1965. It was about three months after I had gotten to Vietnam, and I went to the National Interrogation Center in Saigon. That was a holding prison where important prisoners were brought from around the country. The Rand Corporation had an agreement with the National Interrogation Center to interview prisoners who were held there. So,

91

I went to the National Interrogation Center, looked at the list of prisoners, and we decided that this one prisoner who was— he was an education cadre. A cadre is in the independence movement in Vietnam. A cadre is about the same thing as we would call an officer in the U. S. Army. There were cadre, rank and file, like officers and enlisted men. This man was an education cadre. He specialized in the education of young people. He had joined the movement in 1948 when the war was against the French. He stayed in the movement until he was captured in 1965. His job had been to go around to various villages around Saigon in the provinces surrounding Saigon to teach the young people how to do theater, how to set up group sessions in which they would all write some songs, sing songs, and he was very committed and very sincere. We talked for two days, for two whole days in that cell in that jail in Saigon, and he explained a great deal to me about the presence of America in Vietnam, about what the Vietnamese independence movement was about or what its goals were. It was from him that I first understood what the people in the village think of all this, because the people in the village are the people whose voices are never heard. We very seldom hear from them.

He said that he would—he said that he would never give up. He said that he would never give up no matter how much he was tortured, and he had been tortured very badly because he believed in something.

Now, I had thought up until then that these Viet Cong were indoctrinated fanatics. Well, with that man I learned—and I was to learn later, that there is a difference between indoctrination, fanaticism and a real commitment. I found out really what he was committed to because he told me about how the French had wiped out his entire village, his home village. The French had wiped it out. He told me about how between 1960 and 1965 how his village had been attacked. He explained to me how when a person is indoctrinated or if they're simply brainwashed, then, under very tense situations like when the village is attacked in combat, in very tense situations the indoctrination doesn't mean anything. It falls apart. Unless you really become committed to something—unless you really internalize certain things, then it doesn't do you any good in a tense situation like that. I knew that he was telling me the truth because this man, after many months of being tortured, after sitting there in that jail cell, he, on the second day of the interview —on the second day of the interview we had built up rapport. We liked one another.

On the second day he recited poetry to me. He sang a song to me. He said that that was a poem which he always recited when he got downhearted, and it was a very moving experience. I came to know the Vietnamese people. You see, even now—

(Brief pause.)*

THE COURT: All right, Mr. Russo.

Give him some water.

BY MR. WEINGLASS:

Q   Could you explain briefly the circumstances of your leaving the study?

A   Yes. I left because the result of the study were being altered because the truth about who the Vietnamese people were, the truth about the Vietnamese independence movement were not being told. The reports were being used. They were being used to promote the role of the Air Force. Lies were being told left and right, and I left. . . .

Q   Did you remain in the employ of the Rand Corporation after your return?

A   Yes.

Q   How long did you remain in their employ at the office in Santa Monica?

A   Until January 3, 1969.

---

* At this point Russo was weeping along with many of the spectators in the courtroom.

Q   That would be approximately one year?

A   About that.

Q   During that year in Rand Santa Monica, would you briefly describe the nature of the work that you were doing?

A   Yes. I brought back a great deal of information from Vietnam that I collected during the fall of 1967. It was, for the most part, quantitative numerical information, the agricultural census, in addition to a village census.

When I got back to Rand I took that information and put it on the computer and began to make computer runs for the study that I have already mentioned, the economic and social correlates of government control in South Vietnam.

Q   Now, drawing your attention to the month of May, 1968, did anything of an unusual nature happen in terms of your employment?

A   Yes. I think I was fired from Rand.

Q   When did you finally leave Rand?

A   January, 1969.

Q   During that year at Rand, January '68 to January '69, did you have occasion to see Dan Ellsberg?

A   Yes. My office was right across the hall from Dan's office at Rand, and we spent a great deal of time talking to one another about our experience in Vietnam, and in March of 1968 Dan organized a seminar at Rand around the topic of lessons learned in Vietnam. It was a seminar that was attended by all—most of the people at Rand who had worked on Vietnam research.

Q   Would those seminars meet periodically?

A   Yes. Those seminars met about once a week. . . .

Q   When you left Rand as a full-time employee in January of 1969, did you remain on any capacity with the company?

A   Yes. I remained on the roles as a consultant

94

to the Rand Corporation.

Q Did you know when your consulting role was terminated?

A In August of 1969.

Q Between January 3, 1969 when you left and August of 1969, did you have occasion to render consulting services to the Rand Corporation?

A Yes, I did for one day.

Q Do you know what the security clearance was, the status of it up to the time that you terminated as a consultant?

A Yes. It was top secret.

Q Do you know whether or not your status remained top secret after the time that you were terminated?

A Yes. My understanding was that the security clearance was good for a period of several months after termination. . . .

Russo was next asked to relate his contacts with Daniel Ellsberg after leaving Rand. Russo said his contacts were social.

BY MR. WEINGLASS:

Q Now, in those conversations, did you learn of the work that Dan Ellsberg was doing at the Rand Corporation?

A Yes. He was doing work on lessons learned from Vietnam.

Q Did he indicate to you what materials he was reading in connection with that work?

A Yes. He said he was reading a study that was very interesting.

Q Did he ever reveal to you up to October 1st, 1969 or thereabouts, the name of that study?

A No, he did not.

Q Were you aware of his possessing the McNamara task force study prior to on or about October 1st, 1969?

A No, I was not.

Q   Incidentally, did you know of the existence of that study?

A   Yes, I had learned about the McNamara task force study; that is, the Pentagon Papers in February of 1968 when I came back from Vietnam. I was told by a Rand Corporation Vice President, Gus Shubert, about the existence of the McNamara task force and about the nature of the study that they were doing.

Q   Now, did you ever, between the time you returned from Europe and on or about October 1st, 1969, ask Daniel Ellsberg about the task force study?

A   Yes. I asked him on several occasions about the task force study because I had understood that it was a history of policymaking, a history of decision-making, American decision-making in Vietnam. I was very interested in that topic, and I had asked him on several occasions about this, but he was always unresponsive. He never told me anything about it.

Q   Prior to October 1, 1969, did you know whether or not he had worked himself on the McNamara task force study?

A   No. It came as a surprise. I didn't know he had worked on that task force.

Q   Did there come a time in the month of September, 1969, when you and Dan Ellsberg had a conversation relative to your work in Vietnam?

A   Yes. On the beach in front of his house.

Q   Do you recall who was present?

A   Just he and myself.

Q   Other than the fact of the month of September, . . .

A   I was talking about the experience I had had at the village level in Vietnam, and Dan was talking about the experience he had had at the upper levels of the government, at the decision-making level, and I remarked to Dan that it seemed as though I had seen a very definite pattern of lying and deception, or alteration of the facts throughout the entire experience I had had.

And Dan said that he had had very much the same experience; he was coming to the same conclusion, and that he was reading a study which showed patterns of lying and deception with regard to the U. S. policy in Vietnam.

Q Shortly after that, on or about October 1, 1969, did you have occasion to have another conversation with Dan Ellsberg?

A Yes. One morning he called me up and asked me if I was going to be home; he would like to come over to see me at my house.

Q Did he come over that morning?

A Yes. He came over very shortly after the phone call.

Q Was there anyone else home at your house?

A No.

Q Did you have a conversation?

A Yes.

Q Do you recall the substance of that conversation?

A Yes. Dan said, "Do you know that study I told you about?"

I said, "Yes."

He said, "I want to get it out. Can you arrange for us to Xerox it? Do you know anyone who has a Xerox machine?"

And I said, "Yes, I do, and I will try to arrange it."

Q Do you recall what time of day that conversation took place?

A It was in the late morning.

Q Did Dan Ellsberg have any documents on his person at that time?

A No.

Q Following that conversation, what did you do?

A Following that conversation I called Linda Sinay and asked her if I could use her Xerox machine that night.

Q Who was Linda Sinay?

A She was a person who ran an advertising agency in Los Angeles, and I had had occasion to know her for about six months, and we had done work together.

Q Following the conversation with Linda Sinay, did you have another conversation that same day with Dan Ellsberg?

A Yes. I called Dan back and said that I had arranged to use the Xerox machine that night.

Q Did you subsequently, on that same day, see Dan Ellsberg?

A Yes. We met at the advertising agency and we began to Xerox these documents.

Q Once again, on how many occasions did the copying take place?

A About eight occasions.

Q Who were the persons who were doing the copying?

A Dan, myself, Linda Sinay; on occasion there was Robert Ellsberg, Dan's son, and I believe on occasion there was Mary Ellsberg, Dan's daughter.

Q Now, you mentioned Vu Van Thai this morning. Was he there on more than one occasion?

A He was only there once.

Q Was he copying?

A No.

Q How long did he remain in the premises?

A No longer than an hour. He was waiting for us to go to dinner.

Q Did you all go to dinner that night?

A Yes.

Q Will you indicate to the court and jury just what it was you did on those occasions in connection with the exhibits that are before you?

A Yes. I would take one of these documents (indicating) and hold it on the Xerox machine and copy the contents.

Q Approximately how long a period of time would the documents remain in your hands in that fashion?

A Just while I was using the photocopy machine.

Q To your knowledge did the documents, after they were copied that are before you, the exhibits, leave the Linda Sinay Advertising Agency on the same night in the same condition they were in when they arrived?

A Yes.

MR. WEINGLASS: Your Honor, that completes the direct examination.

(19,097–19,144)

CROSS EXAMINATION

BY MR. NISSEN:

Q Did you read any of the study volumes on the second copying session, sir?

A No. I didn't read any of these volumes. I read copies, but I didn't read any of these volumes.

Q So during the copying sessions, when a copy was produced, you would read that, sir?

A Sometimes. . . .

(19,194)

Q Now, at the time that you and Mr. Ellsberg undertook on October 1 to commence this copying project, you were aware personally that the government has regulations controlling the dissemination of classified documents, weren't you?

MR. BOUDIN: Object, immaterial.

THE COURT: Overruled.

THE WITNESS: I was aware that the executive branch of the government had rules that were very confused because I could never tell the difference between something that is marked "classified" and something that really is classified in the sense that it relates to the national defense.

Now, at the time I wasn't as informed about that as I am now, but I did have some notion of it at that time. . . .

BY MR. NISSEN:

Q Well, sir, did you ever discuss with Mr. Ellsberg any authority that he might have for bringing the exhibits you were copying to Miss Sinay's office?

A Yes.

Q When did that conversation occur?

A We talked on numerous occasions about how, in many contexts, that the agreement to keep secrets about crimes that had been committed was a criminal thing. . . .

Q You did know that Defendant Ellsberg had obtained each of those documents that were being copied from the Rand Corporation?

A I knew that the documents came from the Rand Corporation, yes.

Q And you knew that Defendant Ellsberg had been furnished access to them in connection with official duties he was to be engaged in for the Department of Defense did you not?

MR. BOUDIN: Object to the form, materiality, lack of foundation.

THE COURT: Overruled.

THE WITNESS: I think any American who cared about his country, who knew what we did, would consider it to be an official duty to get these documents to the Congress and to the American people.

MR. NISSEN: We move to strike the answer as

non-responsive, your Honor.

THE COURT: Read the question.

(Question read.)

THE COURT: The answer is stricken.

THE WITNESS: I have problems with the narrow definition of "official duties." For me the duty of an American citizen is total, and it's defined by the Constitution.

THE COURT: The question relates to, at the Rand Corporation, not other duties. . . .

Q At the time of the copying session, sir, you were aware that a person could not be given access to classified material without a security clearance, weren't you?

A Well, Mr. Nissen, I had seen—in Saigon I had seen the government officials give out material that was stamped "classified" to newspapermen all the time. . . .

BY MR. NISSEN:

A Sir, at the time that you participated in the copying sessions, you believed, did you not, that classified material could not be given to a person unless he had a security clearance?

A I believed at the time that the rules were such that we were breaking them, because the rules were designed to serve special interests in the government.

If a government official had some information that was classified that supported what he wanted to do, he would leak it, or he would leak it if it tended to make him look good.

Always in Vietnam the U. S. government was leaking or passing out classified information that would tend to make them look good. If it didn't make them look good, then the strict rules applied and it couldn't be given out.

Everybody knows that who has any contact with the system.

THE COURT: Excuse me. The latter part—

MR. NISSEN: We move to strike the witness'

answer after the statement that he believed the rules were being broken. . . .

    Q You knew at the time that the exhibits which were being copied were handed to you, Miss Sinay, Robert Ellsberg, Mary Ellsberg, and Vu Van Thai, that none of those people, including yourself, had then a security clearance?

    A That is correct. I knew they didn't have a security clearance.

(19,288–19,300)

BY MR. NISSEN:

    Q During court proceedings in this case, sir, you did in the courtroom hand to a government witness, William DePuy, a defense press release accusing him of being a war criminal; did you not, sir?

    A I did, and I do think that General DePuy is a war criminal. I think—

(19,375)

REDIRECT EXAMINATION

BY MR. WEINGLASS:

    Q During any of those occasions at the Linda Sinay Advertising Agency which you have testified about in the fall of 1969, did you and Daniel Ellsberg have a conversation respecting why he took the documents from the safe at the Rand Santa Monica office to the advertising agency?

    A Yes. To get the documents to Senator Fulbright, to the Congress, and ultimately to the American people, because they had a need to know.

(19,381–19,382)

RECROSS EXAMINATION

BY MR. NISSEN:

Q When you said, Mr. Russo, that you didn't believe defendant Ellsberg had stolen the documents, you did believe that he had brought them to Linda Sinay's advertising agency without the authority of anyone, did you not?

A No, that's not a correct statement.

Q You did believe that he was not authorized to copy them, did you not?

A Mr. Nissen, I think he was authorized to copy those documents.

Q Who was it that authorized it, sir?

A I think that the facts speak for themselves; that the documents speak for themselves. When the American government has been keeping secret for 28 years United States policy in Vietnam, I think that speaks for itself. I think the documents speak for themselves, sir. . . .

Q What did you mean by the word "stolen," when you answered that question?

A Depriving the Rand Corporation of their use. If they had been stolen—

THE COURT: That answers the question.

(19,392–19,396)

Daniel Ellsberg followed Anthony Russo to the witness stand. Ellsberg began by recounting his biography up to the time of his involvement with the Pentagon Papers study. At the point we pick up his testimony, he is describing his experiences in Vietnam while working on General Lansdale's senior liaison team.

DANIEL ELLSBERG, SWORN

DIRECT EXAMINATION

BY MR. BOUDIN:

Q   Would you continue describing what you did in Vietnam in performance of your duties.

A   In order to find out—in order to come to understand so that we could improve our policy and our performance and I hoped win this war and beat the Communists for once, as I saw it, I felt that I had—I did begin to drive the roads of Vietnam through every part of the III Corps area, which surrounded Saigon, and then increasingly into IV Corps, the area below Saigon, the Mekong Delta, and by plane and car into the northern II Corps and I Corps area.

I would use the roads by car, visit along the way villages and hamlets. I would sometimes have an interpreter with me or I would speak to officials in French. Most of the officials spoke French, which I did, because the French had occupied Vietnam for seventy years, so I was able to communicate that way.

Increasingly, officials began to speak English, and I could communicate with them.

With the farmers I had to use an interpreter that I carried. I would ask them what the conditions of security were, what they feared, whether the Viet Cong were in that area, what they—what the officials were doing and what they thought of the officials in that area, or, if I was speaking to the officials, what they saw the problems as being.

And in particular I should say I spoke to American advisors who by that time were down to the district

104

level and the battalion levels, a fairly low level, and some of them spoke Vietnamese or had interpreters.

I would write reports on these trips to my boss, General Lansdale, and some of—many of these were forwarded by him to Deputy Ambassador William Porter or to Ambassador Lodge or elsewhere, and I made some other formal reports, in particular one that was meant for the President —a portion of one that was to go to the President in the spring of 1966 based on these field trips that I was making.

I continued the travel because of the discovery that I had made which confirmed a suspicion from the Pentagon that the channels—

THE COURT: Yes, that is unresponsive to the question that is pending. If you will continue on in what you did in furtherance of your duties.

THE WITNESS: Yes.

A I wanted to compare—to compare what I would see with my own eyes along the roads of Vietnam and the hamlets of Vietnam with my own ears speaking to the reporters— I use that word as officials—army people whose main job was reporting really to find out from my own ears what their reporting was and to compare that with what was coming up to headquarters through what I have described as that cable traffic.

I found and reported—. . .

Oh, each of the things, if I may say—explain— each thing that I did was, of course, cleared with, although I often suggested it—but cleared with and had the approval of my boss, and in some cases—Lansdale—and I was loaned by him increasingly to the deputy ambassador for special investigation, so as time went on less of this was at my own initiative and more I was directed to keep driving and keep reporting.

And I reported to them that the fact, as I saw it, that there was a very great divergence between what was to be seen and what the advisers knew, our military advisers knew in the districts and in the battalions and in the platoons, and

105

what was being told by the division advisers or MACV headquarters in writing to their bosses, and higher and higher, and
in fact, second, that there was an increasing divergence, that
the divergence between reality as one saw it with eyes and ears
at the low level got larger as it went up, larger and larger.

So that I—so that, as I informed former supe-
riors in Washington and I informed them directly in writing, I
could now understand the feeling that had lead me to Vietnam
that you could not learn about Vietnam from the cables.

(19,526–19,530)

BY MR. BOUDIN:

Q   Will you state to the Court and to the jury
how you came to work on that project. By "that project"
I mean the task force report.

A   I was invited by Dr. Morton Halperin, who
had been named—put in charge of the report, to join the task
force. I can't remember the exact time that he asked me because
it was during the summer, and I wasn't able immediately
to comply, but I began work as of about late September or early
October 1967.

Q   Were you given specific instructions by Dr.
Halperin and by one of his subordinates as to what your work
was to be?

A   Yes, by Dr. Leslie Gelb, who was immediately
in charge of producing the report.

Q   And what—

A   He was the deputy to Mr. Halperin.

Q   And what were those instructions?

A   The instructions were to produce a first
draft of a portion of this historical account of decision-making.
He said that I could choose any area that I wanted particularly,
and I chose the 1961 period of the early decisions by President
Kennedy to do research on.

(19,600–19,601)

106

Ellsberg went on to recount in detail the now familiar circumstances surrounding his gaining access to the Pentagon Papers study and his transporting and use of the volumes while at Rand. His account corroborated other defense witnesses' testimony as to the mechanics of his use of and access to the documents and his keeping the volumes out of Rand's top secret control system at Santa Monica according to the agreement Morton Halperin testified about earlier.

BY MR. BOUDIN:

Q Did you tell Mr. Russo prior to September 30, 1969, of the existence of those volumes?

A No, I did not.

Q Did you tell Miss Linda Sinay—

THE COURT: Clarify one thing: When you say "those volumes", what do you mean?

THE WITNESS: The explanation specifically with Mr. Russo, your Honor, would be that I had discussed in general terms with him and others at Rand the existence of a study which I did not name or describe in any detail.

To my knowledge he had no way of inferring anything about this particular study as being the same one that I had described to him.

THE COURT: The latter part of the answer about what he may or may not have had any way of knowing will be stricken. The first part remains. All right.

BY MR. BOUDIN:

Q Did you tell Mr. Russo prior to September 30, 1969, that the volumes which you received on March 3, 1969, set forth in receipts 30 and 31, had been at the Rand office in Washington, D. C.?

A No, I did not.

Q Did you tell Miss Sinay that?

A No, I didn't.

Q Did you tell Mr. Vu Van Thai that prior to September 30, 1969?

A   No, I didn't.

(19,718–19,719)

Q   In connection with which of your duties were you reading Exhibits 1 through 18, the task force volumes which you have just referred to?

A   That was also in connection with my duties on the "Lessons for Vietnam" project. I read the studies, took notes on questions that they raised or questions that they answered in a smaller number of cases, and patterns that they suggested with respect to our decision making, high-level decision making in Vietnam over the period from '45 to '68.

I incorporated these—some of these conclusions in the draft memoranda that I have mentioned earlier, of which I think I wrote nine by July of 1969. So several of those did have conclusions and/or ideas or questions that had been suggested to me by reading the task force volumes, and that was the purpose for which I was reading them.

Of course, the ultimate objective was finished RM's of this sort, but meanwhile I was giving the results directly to officials from the Pentagon, from the Advanced Research Projects Agency, and other officials, some from International Security Affairs who came through Rand in July—June and July.

Q   At the end of September 1969 did you take any action with respect to the Government's Exhibits 1 through 20?

A   Yes.

Q   When did you take such action?

A   On the evening of September 30—well, perhaps I should start in the morning. In the morning, with respect to these volumes, I went to the home of Tony Russo in Santa Monica, told him—reminded him of the study that I described earlier in very general terms, told him that I had copies of it, that it was marked "Classified," that I had a copy of it in my safe at the Rand Corporation, and that I wanted to get it—some information to the Congress, and that I needed to copy those copies.

I asked him if he had access to a Xerox machine, and he said he thought he might be able to find one.

Later that afternoon I was informed by him that he had found a Xerox machine at the office of a friend, and that night I took several of the volumes from my safe at the top secret——my top secret safe at the Rand Corporation, took them in to the Linda Sinay Advertising Agency on Melrose, having been given the address by Tony, and we proceeded to copy several of the documents. . . .

       Q Why did you take the actions which you just described?

       MR. NISSEN: Objection, immaterial.

       THE COURT: Sustained.

                   (19,742–19,745)

BY MR. BOUDIN:

       Q Did you then, Dr. Ellsberg, at Miss Sinay's office, copy Exhibits 1 through 20?

       A On a succession of nights, yes, I did—either I or friends helping me.

       Q And did you return them to the Rand Santa Monica office?

       A Yes. In each case I returned them—the volume on the next working day after I had taken them out.

       Q Was copying of any of those documents ever done when you were not in the Sinay office and present?

       A No. I was always present.

       Q Were there ever any instances when anyone other than you took Exhibits 1 through 20 away from the Sinay office after Xeroxing or copying?

       A No. On each occasion I took them back.

       Q Were there ever any occasions on which you

did not return Exhibits 1 through 20 to Rand on the first work day after Xeroxing?

A No. . . .

Q During the time that Mr. Vu Van Thai was present in the advertising agency of Miss Sinay on October 4, 1969, did you read any of the task force—I'm sorry—did he read any of the exhibits in the group, Government's Exhibits 1 through 20?

THE WITNESS: Yes, I showed him several pages of one, and he thumbed briefly through the rest of that volume. That was the only one that he handled. . . .

BY MR. BOUDIN:

Q Dr. Ellsberg, were your children present during any part of the copying of Exhibits 1 through 20?

A My children were present, yes. Robert was present on two occasions and Mary was present on—my daughter was present on one occasion along with Robert. . . .

Q Would you tell us what Robert did while he was there?

A Robert helped on both nights, I think, that he was there, one of which was mostly an afternoon, a Saturday afternoon—helped Xerox some of the papers, and I think that was primarily all that he did, and Mary, on the evening that she was there, briefly helped cut off the top secret marking from the copies—of some of the copies that were made with a scissors or a paper slicer.

Q Did you take any other steps to remove the top secret markings?

A Yes. Yes, I used the method described earlier of putting strips of cardboard over the top and bottom of the Xerox screen so that the top secret marking on the original would not come through on the copy that was made.

Q And why did you do that?

A I expected that in order to get it to a number of members of Congress I would need more than one copy, one or two copies, and for that purpose I would have to use one of them to make copies from a commercial copying establishment, and that it would raise questions if I asked a commercial firm to copy something that had classification markings on it.

So I wanted a copy that had no markings on it. . . .

BY MR. BOUDIN:

Q   On October 3, 1969, did you know or believe that Exhibits 1 through 20 contained information, the disclosure of which could injure the national defense of the United States?

A   I believed'—I would say that I knew that not a page of those exhibits could injure the national defense if disclosed to anyone, and had I believed otherwise I would not have copied it.

Q   Would you state whether there were any other reasons for your belief that the disclosure of the information could not injure the United States?

A   Yes.

Q   Please do.

A   It seemed—I believed that disclosure of the fact revealed in these papers, the pattern, that the policy of the United States could not be improved simply by getting better information to the President, because the President had had adequate information.

And the revelation of that fact, which was—I learned from the Pentagon Papers and which contradicted what I had believed earlier, that couldn't injure the United States.

And that the revelation of the fact that if Congress really had the information it needed to make wise decisions, if only it realized that there were no super secrets somewhere else that gave a good reason for what we were doing, that there were no good reasons hidden in those Pentagon Papers for what we were doing, that might give Congress this self-confidence to act to end the war, and that could not damage any of the institutions or the people of the United States who were being damaged by the war.

(19,755–19,806)

   The defense at this point in Ellsberg's direct testimony wanted to have Ellsberg testify to the effect that he had a meeting with Senator Fulbright in which Fulbright was made aware of the existence of the task force volumes and negotiations begun on whether the documents could be used in Senate hearings. The defense also wanted to prove that copies of the Pentagon Papers were actually given to Senator Fulbright by Ellsberg. Judge Byrne ruled that this line of testimony was immaterial to the issues before the court.

CROSS EXAMINATION

BY MR. NISSEN:

   Q   And with regard to each of the 20, you had obtained possession or custody of them with regard to duties that you had at Rand, correct?

   A   That is correct.

   Q   Those duties involved certain projects that you had mentioned on direct examination, sir?

   A   Yes.

   Q   You had no permission from anyone to remove the documents from the Rand premises to Miss Sinay's advertising agency, did you, sir?. . .

   A   No one had given me such permission.

BY MR. NISSEN:

   Q   Yes. The part that is filled in on the form is the Part 1?

   A   Right. Yes.

   Q   And that part bears your handwritten signature, or your signature?

A   Yes, it does.

Q   In the statement to which you have put your signature it says, in part—well, perhaps, your Honor, would the witness read aloud the statement that you have signed.

THE COURT: Starting where?

MR. NISSEN: Starting, "I hereby certify. . . "

THE COURT: All right.

MR. BOUDIN: I object, your Honor. The document is in evidence. It speaks for itself.

THE COURT: Overruled.

BY THE WITNESS:

"I hereby certify that I have received a security briefing. I shall not knowingly and willfully communicate, deliver, or transmit in any manner classified information to an unauthorized person or agency. I am informed that such improper disclosure may be punishable under federal criminal statutes. I have been instructed in the importance of classified information, and in the procedure governing its safeguarding. I am informed that willful violation or disregard of security violations may cause the loss of my security clearance. I have read or have had read to me the portions of the espionage laws and other federal criminal statutes relating to the safeguarding of classified information, reproduced in Appendix 6, Department of Defense Industrial Security Manual. I will report to the Federal Bureau of Investigation and to my employer, without delay, any incident which I believe to constitute an attempt to solicit classified information by any unauthorized person."

BY MR. NISSEN:

Q   Thank you. Now with regard to the—

A   Excuse me. It is dated September 11, 1967.

113

Q With regard to the portion that you read stating, "I have read or have had read to me the portions of the espionage laws and other federal criminal statutes relating to the safeguarding of classified information." et cetera, at that time, sir, which is September '67, had you read again or read at all the espionage laws and other federal criminal statutes referred to?

A Well, I don't—no portion of the espionage law comes to mind relating to classified information, other than one that is not in this case—and I think that was not read to me—having to do with government employees.

The answer is there are no portions of the espionage laws applying to people at Rand that refer to classified information, so I can't recall what my state of mind was when I wrote that, when I signed that. Confused, probably.

BY MR. NISSEN:

Q Had you read portions of the espionage laws at that time, regardless of what you think they related to?

A Yes.

(19,937–20,014)

BY MR. NISSEN:

Q On or about July 1, 1971, did you orally state, sir, at a press conference in Cambridge, Massachusetts, in substance, that you did not release the negotiating volumes because you did not want to contribute to the possibility of getting in the way of the U. S. negotiations?

MR. WEINGLASS: Objection on the same ground.

MR. BOUDIN: Same ground.

BY MR. NISSEN:

Q Did you on or about that date make a statement, in substance, as I had asked you?

A In the course of the year I have addressed questions as to why I gave that to the Senate Foreign Relations

Committee and made only one copy and gave it to them, and I could not recall any given occasion.

Now, if the period of time is the last year or so, I would be happy to say what I answer to that question when I am generally asked it, which is often, what I recall saying on many occasions. I don't remember any specific occasion.

Q   With regard, sir. to the—

A   I am not denying that I addressed that subject. . . .

Q   At the time that you were copying the exhibits in Linda Sinay's office, sir, you were of the belief that your doing so was in violation of Section 793*; were you not?

A   Certainly not.

Q   You have made the statement on several occasions over the past many months that at that time you believed you were violating the law—

MR. BOUDIN: Excuse me, your Honor. I object to this question and—

THE COURT: Sustained.

(20,109–20,115)

BY MR. NISSEN:

Q   And one of the types of material that you find in the Pentagon Papers is evidence of a conspiracy by United States officials to secretly plan and wage aggressive war against North Vietnam; true, sir?

A   Well, I tried to correct that. I think that is imprecise and misleading language. And I usually use the term on that subject, about the describing the experience that I had directly in the Pentagon, and these other episodes, but speaking now only from my personal knowledge in the Pentagon, that I tried to contribute to the volumes, I have spoken of a conspir-

---

* This refers to a section of the law cited in the espionage counts in the indictment.

115

atorial style, distinguishing that from a conspiracy in which any individual meant harm to this country or to others.

On the contrary, the evidence seemed to be that they meant for the best of this country, of the country as they saw it, and even the best for world peace in what they were doing.

But they acted in a conspiratorial manner, in the sense that they did not tell the public what they were doing.

To the contrary, they denied what they were doing, day by day, and publicly and to the Congress.

They described it in other terms. They consciously—and I was, of course, part of this, in a lowly way, in a kind of high paid clerk way, not to reduce my responsibility or exaggerate it.

But in which I was quite conscious of the efforts taken to mislead Congress and the public as to what we were doing in '64 and '65, I am speaking now, and to carry out actions, in which a lot of people were going to die, for whatever motives, to do so knowing that if it were fully known what they were doing, even though, let's say we or the people I worked with thought that it was the best, it was for the best of the country, but knowing that if they said frankly what they were doing, the majority of the country wouldn't agree with it, and wouldn't allow them, wouldn't give them the resources or the authority to do it.

And that is why it had to be kept secret from the American public, even while what we were doing was of course directly known to the people on whom the bombs were falling, or in some cases people to whom we expained it directly, as in the Seaborn case where we told Pham Van Dong through Seaborn what we were doing, even during an election campaign, when the American people were told by the opposing candidate that we should make such threats—Goldwater—and the incumbent said we should not, it would be illegal, it would be irresponsible, it would be crazy, even while he was giving Seaborn the directions to do so. . . .

That I knew at the time that the people that I worked for and with, and who were descibed in these documents, in some cases with minor help by me, were patriotic men who wanted the best for this country.

And so the word conspirator—

THE COURT: Just the documents.

THE WITNESS: I say that to say that the word conspirator, your Honor, conveys an implication of conscious wrongdoing, which would be incorrect.

And if I ever used that word hastily or sloppily, it is misleading.

But I think the word conspiratorial, meaning as if in a conspiracy, as if they were doing something wrong, that they shouldn't be doing, that the people wouldn't want them to know, that that seemed to me not only an accurate word, but it came to me as a puzzle.

This is, as a researcher, I set out to read the Pentagon Papers, having lived through the period. I set out to read them to come to understand that.

This was a phenomenon. Why did they act that way? If they were doing what they knew was good—why did they keep it a secret?

(20,119–20,130)

With Ellsberg's testimony completed the defense was ready to rest its case and did so after its final witness,Richard A. Falk, Professor of International Law at Princeton University, when the court ruled that Professor Falk would not be allowed to testify as to whether or not a person possessing the information contained in the Pentagon Papers study would be reasonable in his belief that he possessed possible evidence of an infraction of international law.

Questions for Analysis and
Jury Deliberation

THE DEFENSE'S CASE

WEINGLASS' OPENING STATEMENT
(Pages 62–117)

1. What is Mr. Weinglass' definition of theft and view as to what elements of the crime the government must prove?
2. What difference is there between the government's case against Russo and its case against Ellsberg according to Weinglass in his opening statement?
3. Weinglass makes a distinction between the taking of the original government documents and making or producing xerox copies. What is the issue involved in this distinction? Is the distinction credible?
4. Does Mr. Weinglass provide a clue to the defense's strategy in his earlier cross-examination of Mr. Bartimo and Mr. Nesson's and Mr. Young's cross-examination of Ms. Butler?
5. What theory does Mr. Weinglass advance in his opening statement as to why the documents were taken by Ellsberg and xeroxed by Ellsberg and Russo? How does the defense theory differ in any respect from Mr. Boudin's theory of the case advanced in his earlier opening statement?
6. Is Mr. Weinglass' argument that the taking and xeroxing of the documents while not authorized by RAND could not amount to a violation of law but only a violation of an employer's rules convincing? What assumptions underlie this argument?
7. How does Weinglass imply that Ellsberg and Russo have already paid a heavy price for violating their employer's rules?

8. Why does Mr. Weinglass mention in closing his opening statement that Russo did believe he was violating the law at the time he helped Ellsberg xerox the documents?

HALPERIN TESTIMONY
(Pages 71–84)

1. What is the significance of Dr. Halperin's testimony that the existence of the Pentagon Papers task force study was originally meant to be kept secret from the Department of Defense, the Department of State, the White House, the U. S. Military Assistance Command in Vietnam, members of Congress and the general public?
2. What justification does Dr. Halperin give for taking the Pentagon Papers study with him along with Mr. Warnke and Mr. Gelb upon leaving the government services? Was Dr. Halperin authorized to take the study and place it in storage with RAND?
3. Were the terms of the storage arrangement with RAND according to Halperin's testimony consistent with the prior testimony of Best and Butler?
4. What significance can be attributed to the fact that Mr. Rowen and Mr. Henderson of RAND agreed to store the documents for Halperin, Warnke and Gelb and not to enter the documents in RAND's Top Security Control System? Does RAND's action support the defense's view that Halperin owned the Pentagon Papers?
5. Is there a reason given why Daniel Ellsberg's initial requests to gain access to the study were denied by Halperin? Why was access finally granted?
6. Is Halperin's distinction between taking the Pentagon Papers home and having them shipped to RAND and stored responsive to Mr. Nissen's questions whether he was authorized to retain the Papers after leaving his job in the Department of Defense?
7. Does the fact that other officials may have taken classified documents with them upon leaving their government jobs justify or authorize Halperin's putting the Pentagon Papers documents in storage with RAND?
8. What significance should be attached to Dr. Halperin's admissions on cross-examination that he on more than one occasion refused to answer questions put to him by the FBI about his

knowledge of how information about the Wheeler Report was leaked to the New York Times?

9. What significance should be attached to the fact that Halperin is a full-time, paid consultant to Ellsberg and Russo's defense team? Does Halperin evince a bias in favor of the defense in his testimony?

TESTIMONY OF ANTHONY RUSSO
(Pages 85–103)

1. What is the effect of Russo's admission that he assisted in the xeroxing of the documents? Can xeroxing a document be considered "stealing," ie., the willful taking and carrying away of the property of another, without right and without leave or consent of the owner?

2. Is Russo's testimony regarding his work for RAND in Vietnam on the research memorandum called "Some Findings of the Viet Cong Motivation and Morale Study" relevant to the issue whether or not he stole the Pentagon Papers or received stolen property? What is the purpose of this testimony?

3. What point is Russo trying to make by reciting his interview with the man referred to as file number AG132? Is this an attempt to sway the jury by an appeal to emotion?

4. To what extent does Russo indicate he made an agreement to copy the documents with Ellsberg?

5. What significance can be attached to the fact that Russo's girl friend, Linda Sinay, and others assisted in the xeroxing?

6. What distinction is Russo trying to make in his answer on cross-examination that he did not read any of the original documents and that he read only the xerox copies? Is the distinction a meaningful one?

7. What significance should be attached to Russo's admission that he handed one of the prosecution witnesses, General William De Puy, a press release in the court room which accused the general of being a war criminal? Does such conduct by a defendant have any effect on your ability to judge his guilt or innocence for theft as charged?

8. What significance should be attached to Russo's admission that he believed that it was unlawful at the time of the xeroxing to give xeroxed classified material to persons like Ms. Sinay and

Vu Van Thai to read when he knew they did not have security clearances?

TESTIMONY OF DANIEL ELLSBERG
(Pages 104–117)

1. Does Daniel Ellsberg's testimony about his activities while an adviser to General Lansdale in Vietnam provide a partial motive for why he wanted to copy and disseminate the Pentagon Papers study?
2. Does Ellsberg's account of his initial contacts with Russo, Ms. Sinay and others differ in any way from Russo's and Sinay's accounts?
3. What significance should be attached to fact that Ellsberg handed a volume of the original Pentagon Papers study to Vu Van Thai who thumbed through it during the copying session?
4. What significance should be attached to Ellsberg's testimony that he had his son and daughter help him with the xeroxing and help him to remove the top secret markings from the copies made?
5. What significance should be attached to Ellsberg's belief that the disclosure of the information in the documents he xeroxed could not injure the United States?
6. Did Ellsberg's desire to turn the Pentagon Papers study over to Senator Fullbright's committee so that the study could be made public through hearing of the Senate Foreign Relations Committee justify his actions?
7. What is the effect of Mr. Nissen's cross-examination on the issue whether Ellsberg had authority to take the documents from RAND?
8. What is the significance of the agreements Ellsberg signed with the RAND Corporation? Do these agreements give the government control over a RAND employee's misuse of classified information?
9. Why would Mr. Nissen want to ask Dr. Ellsberg whether the Pentagon Papers in his opinion contained evidence of a conspiracy by the United States to secretly plan and wage war against North Vietnam? Is Ellsberg's answer relevant to the theft charge?

WRITING ASSIGNMENTS

1. Prepare an outline or abstract of the case for the prosecution and defense based on the opening statements.
2. Research the history of RAND Corporation and trace its interesting relationship to the United States government.
3. Use the definitions of theft in the preceeding section to outline the government's case that it had to prove. Did the government successfully prove all the necessary elements?
4. Summarize the evidence that argues for the conviction of Russo and Ellsberg on the theft charge. Summarize the evidence that argues for acquittal. Write your recommendations as to which side's evidence is more compelling and indicate why.

Bibliography

Suggested Readings:

BOOKS:
1. Ellsberg, Daniel, *Papers On The War*, Simon & Schuster (1972).
2. *Hearings Before The Select Committee On Presidential Campaign Activities Of The United States Senate*, vols. 6, 7, U.S. Government Printing Office, Washington, D.C. (1973).
3. *The Pentagon Papers* as Published by THE NEW YORK TIMES, Bantam Books, (1971).

ARTICLES:
1. Bendat, James R., "The Indictment of Anthony Russo," *New Republic*, May 27, 1972.
2. Farred, Barry, "The Ellsberg Mask," *Harpers*, October, 1973.
3. Russo, Anthony, "Inside the RAND Corporation And Out: My Story," *Ramparts*, April, 1972.
4. Schrag, Peter, "The Ellsberg Affair," *Saturday Review*, November 13, 1971.
5. Terkel, Studs, "Servants Of The State — A Conversation With Daniel Ellsberg,"*Harpers*, February, 1972.